KEYS TO INVESTING IN COMMON STOCKS

Second Edition

Barbara Apostolou, Ph.D., C.P.A.
Associate Professor
Louisiana State University

Nicholas G. Apostolou, D.B.A., C.P.A.
Professor
Louisiana State University

BARRON'S

© Copyright 1995 by Barron's Educational Series, Inc.
Prior edition © Copyright 1990 by Barron's Educational Series, Inc.

All inquiries should be addressed to:
Barron's Educational Series, Inc.
250 Wireless Boulevard
Hauppauge, NY 11788

Library of Congress Catalog Card Number 94-39465

International Standard Book Number 0-8120-9004-7

Library of Congress Cataloging-in-Publication Data

Apostolou, Barbara.
    Keys to investing in common stocks / Barbara Apostolou, Nicholas
    G. Apostolou.— 2nd ed.
        p. cm.
    Includes index.
    ISBN 0-8120-9004-7
1. Stocks—United States—handbooks, manuals, etc.—
I. Apostolou, Nicholas G. II. Title.
HG4921.A55 1995   94-39465
33263′223—dc20   CIP

PRINTED IN THE UNITED STATES OF AMERICA

5678   9770   98765432

TABLE OF CONTENTS

1

WHAT IS COMMON STOCK?

The 1990s continue to provide excellent opportunities for investors to profit from owning shares of common stock. The economy recovered from the recession of 1990-91, inflation continued subdued, and the stock market reached new heights. Has this performance stilled the voices of the naysayers? Hardly. Many so-called experts are predicting disaster for the economy and the stock market. In addition, reported abuses by insiders and traders have made many investors uneasy. How should the individual investor react? Very simply, every investor should focus on the long term. The American economy will continue to grow, and corporations will continue to prosper. Common stock ownership gives investors a direct stake in the future of corporations. Ownership of common stock has proved over many years to be one of the best ways for investors to earn money. Even those investors with limited capital are not shut out of this market.

Common stock represents shares of ownership in a corporation. Its owners bear the ultimate risk of loss and reap the benefits of success. Neither dividends nor assets upon dissolution are guaranteed to common stockholders. Nonetheless, they are owners of the corporation and will profit the most if the company is successful. The most popular way to invest in corporations is to own shares of common stock. More than 50 million people currently own stock in publicly traded companies.

Comparing investments. A successful investor should possess a sense of history. And history tends to repeat itself, although not exactly in the same form. Markets are volatile, prices will fluctuate, but investors should be aware that opportunities are greatest when general pessimism prevails. On the other hand, a cautious stance generally should be assumed when the investment community is most optimistic. Looking at past trends in the markets assists in maintaining objectivity and a sense of perspective. An additional advantage is that alternative investments can be compared over time.

In the period from 1926–1993 common stocks increased at an average annual rate of over 10%, substantially exceeding the return from long-term government bonds (5.0%) and U.S. Treasury bills (3.7%). Inflation over this 67-year period averaged 3% annually. If one dollar was invested in common stock in 1926 (measured by using Standard & Poor's [S&P] Composite Index and assuming all dividends were reinvested), the investment would have accumulated to $800.08 at the end of 1993. Meanwhile, one dollar invested in long-term government bonds would have grown to $28.03, while a dollar invested in Treasury bills would have increased to $11.73.

The evidence is compelling that in the long run investments in common stock have outperformed investments in the other capital markets. Although investors in common stock assume greater risk than those who invest in government bonds, clearly their returns over the years have been much greater.

Finally, an issuance of a caveat is appropriate. The returns from common stock investments result from averaging the returns from many stocks. Poor choices of stocks can lead to losses even when the stock market is rising. Thus the successful investor must be willing to expend the time and effort to select quality stocks and to be diversified. Don't count on having the next Microsoft; no one can predict the future, and you might decide to invest in, say, the steel industry just before it has another fall from power. Many publications and advisory services are available to assist the investor (see Key 24). In addition, investors can purchase mutual funds which offer the twin advantages of professional management and diversification.

2

ASSET ALLOCATION

Most investors believe that the most important investing decision they make is the selection of individual stocks, bonds, mutual funds, and so forth. However, these decisions are not nearly as important as generally assumed.

The asset allocation decision—how you split your dollars among stocks, bonds, and cash (including money market funds and short-term CDs)—is by far the most important determinant of investment performance. It turns out that what portion of your total assets is invested in stocks is generally more significant than the individual stocks you select.

Although the importance of asset allocation over individual security selection may surprise you, this statement is not news to research academics. A study by Brinson, Singer, and Beebower (published in the May-June 1991 issue of *Financial Analysts Journal*) assessed the performance of 82 large pension funds over a ten-year period. Their research shows that asset allocation determines more than 90% of the total return. The individual stocks, bonds, and other assets that the pension funds picked did little on average to improve performance over the ten-year period.

Many financial newsletters in recent years have increasingly recognized asset allocation as a positive approach to investment. Although it might be perceived as a gimmick to sell financial products, those newsletters are onto something investors can ignore only at their peril.

Most investors tend to pay little or no attention to how they allocate their assets. All too often, they own a hodgepodge of mutual funds or common stock bought at various times without consideration of how they complement each other. That is a big mistake. Proper attention to asset allocation can enable you to substantially reduce your risk with little or no decrease in return.

The 25-year compound annual returns (1969–1993), including price changes and reinvested dividends, for common stock (as measured by the Standard & Poor's 500 Index) is 10.5%. But the average return masks some years of glittering returns and other years that were real downers.

Total returns soared more than 30% in five of the years but stocks were losing investments in six other years, including the 26.47% plunge in 1974. Some investors may not be comfortable with this level of volatility or risk. Those investors who plan to cash in their stocks to finance the college education of their children or for their retirement in a few years may find the possibility of a 26.47% plunge unacceptable.

That's where asset allocation comes in. Consider what would have happened if an investor had put a third of his or her money in stocks, a third in Treasury bonds, and a third in a cash equivalent investment such as Treasury bills. In the 25-year period, that investor would have lost money only four times, and the largest loss would have been less than 5%. Meanwhile, the compound annual return would have been about 9%, compared with 10.5% for an all-stock portfolio. Thus, historically, sacrificing a 1.5% total return has been accompanied by dramatically reduced risk.

If you are interested in making the most money possible, and your time horizon is 30 to 40 years, then investing entirely in stocks makes sense. Although you have a 30% chance of loss in any one-year period (based upon results over the last 60 years), your risk drops to 15% over any five-year holding period and only 4% in any ten-year period. In other words, extending the amount of time invested in the stock market greatly reduces risk.

But most investors have shorter time horizons, and investing totally in stocks is too risky. For them, investing in several classes of assets such as stocks, bonds, real estate (at least your own home), and cash equivalents is a better approach.

Because your asset mix is so important, some mutual fund companies now offer free services to help investors design their portfolios. These companies include Dreyfus Corporation (800-645-6561), T. Rowe Price Associates (800-638-5360), Fidelity Investments (800-544-8888), and SteinRoe Mutual Funds (800-338-2550). They will either suggest an allocation if you complete a questionnaire or provide a worksheet that enables you to figure out your own mix.

The best mix of investments will vary depending upon your age, income, health, employment stability, family size, and tolerance of risk. Each investor has to structure a strategy that fits his or her own personal circumstances, and this strategy will change as you get older and your financial position changes.

As a general rule, the further you are from your investment goal, the more you should have in stocks. The closer you get to that goal, the more you can allocate to bonds and money market instruments, such as Treasury bills.

One simple but effective approach to common stock investment uses the following formula: subtract your age from 100. That amount represents the percentage of your portfolio you should put into stocks. For example, this formula means that a 40-year-old should have 60% of holdings in stocks.

When looking at how your assets are allocated, consider all your investments, including real estate, brokerage accounts, 401(K) money, individual retirement accounts, and certificates of deposit. Once you have settled on the mix of investments you desire, you should seek to maintain the targeted percentage for your mix of assets. To accomplish this goal, you should compute your allocation at least once a year. Because of a downturn in the stock market, you could discover that stocks are a smaller percentage of your portfolio than you desire. In that case, you should put more into stocks and lighten up on your other investments.

In making these asset allocation decisions, it helps to have an overview of how the three major categories (stocks, bonds, and cash equivalents) have performed historically. Stock and bond averages and indexes can provide this perspective.

Current index information is readily available in local and national newspapers and magazines. The best periodical for historical information remains the weekly publication *Barron's* (800-228-6262).

The most complete information giving year-by-year total returns from 1926 for various stock and bond groups, as well as compound annual returns for different holding periods, is the yearly book *Stock, Bonds, Bills, and Inflation* published by Ibbotson Associates (312-616-1620). The 1994 yearbook costs $90. This publication is available at many libraries.

3

STOCK EXCHANGES

Common stocks are traded primarily on nine stock exchanges in the United States. The largest stock exchange is the New York Stock Exchange (NYSE), which lists over 2400 companies with more than 140 billion shares issued and a market value of about $4.5 trillion. A smaller version of the NYSE is the American Stock Exchange (AMEX), which is also located in Manhattan's financial district. The NYSE and AMEX are considered national exchanges. Common stock is also traded on seven major regional exchanges.

Generally, the stocks of the largest companies are traded on the NYSE, whereas those of the smaller companies are traded on the AMEX. The regional exchanges trade stocks of local corporations as well as stocks listed on the NYSE and AMEX. The NYSE and AMEX are generally considered national in scope because of the large number of securities listed, the geographical dispersion of the firms, and the clientele they serve.

New York Stock Exchange. The NYSE dates back to 1817, when brokers adopted a constitution creating the New York Stock and Exchange Board, the predecessor of today's Big Board. This constitution outlined membership requirements and commission rates and established procedures for trading and settling transactions. The brokers met in what was called a "call" market. Two times a day the president of the Board read the list of securities and members shouted bids and offers from their assigned chairs. Thus the origin of the term "seat," which continues to signify membership on the NYSE.

The number of shares listed as well as the number of shares traded on the Exchange have increased steadily through the years. Prior to the 1960s, the average daily trading volume was less than 3 million shares. Daily volume averaged about 15 million shares during the first half of the 1970s and exceeded 30 million by the end of that decade. Volume exploded during the 1980s with daily volume usually exceeding 100 million shares. On October 20, 1987, a record 608,120,000 shares were traded on the NYSE. In the 1990s, volume has continued to surge, with daily trading averaging over 250 million shares in 1994.

Stock exchange specialists are the center of the auction market for stocks. Their role is critical in maintaining an orderly market for stocks. The specialist is a member of the exchange who has been assigned responsibility for about 15 different stocks. He or she must possess substantial capital and the knowledge to carry out this responsibility. Currently, there are about 435 specialists on the floor of the NYSE.

The requirements for listing on the NYSE are more stringent than the requirements on the other exchanges. A company must meet or exceed specified levels of net earnings, assets, and trading volume, and its shares must be widely held by investors. In addition, the NYSE requires evidence that trading interest in the company's shares is sufficient. Finally, a prospective listee must also agree to meet standards of disclosure, corporate governance, and shareholder participation.

American Stock Exchange. The AMEX was begun by a group of individuals who traded unlisted shares at an outdoor location referred to as the Outdoor Curb Market. Typically, AMEX firms are smaller and younger than the firms listed on the NYSE. These companies are frequently considered emerging growth companies—companies that are not quite seasoned enough for the Big Board. Another characteristic of the AMEX is the number of smaller energy companies listed; the speculative nature of these stocks tends to make prices on the AMEX more volatile than those on the NYSE.

Trading volume on the AMEX typically varies from 5% to 7% of that on the NYSE. On October 20, 1987, a record volume of 43,432,760 shares traded on the AMEX. The disparity between the activity on the two exchanges is even greater when measured by the value of trading because the price of shares on the NYSE tends to be higher than that of shares on the AMEX.

Regional exchanges. Originally, these exchanges traded the securities of the regional companies located in their areas—thus the origin of the name. However, the development of rapid communication expanded their scope. As a result, stocks on the NYSE and AMEX are traded as well as local stocks. For example, IBM and General Motors are both listed on the NYSE, but they are also listed on several regional exchanges. This dual listing permits local brokerage firms that are not members of the NYSE to trade shares of dual-listed stock using their membership on a regional exchange. As a result, the local broker does not have to forgo part of the commission by trading through the NYSE. Most of the volume on regional exchanges currently results from trading in dual-listed issues.

The largest of the regional exchanges is the Midwest Stock Exchange (MSE), located in Chicago. The MSE is a result of the merger of the Chicago, Cleveland, Minneapolis-St. Paul, St. Louis, and, in 1960, the New Orleans Stock Exchange. Its trading activity now exceeds that of the AMEX, making it the second largest organized stock exchange in the United States.

Other prominent regional exchanges include:

> Pacific Stock Exchange
> Philadelphia Stock Exchange
> Boston Stock Exchange
> Cincinnati Stock Exchange

4

OVER-THE-COUNTER MARKET

The term over-the-counter (OTC) originated when securities were traded over the counters in the storefront offices of various dealers from their inventory of securities. However, the term is currently an inaccurate description of how securities are traded in this market. The OTC market does not have centralized trading floors where all orders are processed as do the NYSE and the AMEX. Instead, trading is conducted through a centralized computer-telephone network linking dealers across the country. Thus, these dealers can negotiate directly with one another and with customers.

The OTC market is based on a number of dealers buying and selling securities for their own accounts. The number of dealers that make a market in a particular security depends upon the popularity and the size of the issue. Each dealer making a market purchases securities from sellers at a bid price while selling to buyers at a higher asked price. The difference between the bid and asked price is the spread that represents the dealer's profit.

When an investor trades OTC, an order is presented to a broker. If the broker acts as a dealer in that security, the broker will fill the order from inventory. Otherwise, the broker will act as an agent in contacting the dealer who offers the best price. The broker usually charges a commission for finding the dealer who makes a market in the security.

Securities traded. The OTC market is a huge market that includes about 20,000 securities. Although OTC stocks represent many small and unseasoned companies, the range of securities traded is actually great. The types of securities traded include common and preferred stocks, corporate bonds, U.S. government securities, municipal bonds, options and warrants, and foreign securities. There are several reasons why some securities are represented in the OTC market rather than being listed on one of the exchanges. Some securities issued by smaller companies cannot meet the more stringent requirements of the exchanges. Unseasoned issues of smaller companies typically are traded in the OTC market. Some of these will eventually qualify for listing on one of the exchanges.

In other cases, firms choose to have their securities traded in the OTC market even though they could fulfill the requirements for listing on the exchanges. Sometimes this occurs because management prefers the negotiated OTC market, with its multiple dealers making a market in stocks, rather than the specialist system offered by the organized exchanges. Other companies may wish to avoid the financial disclosure and reporting requirements required by the exchanges. For instance, many large financial institutions continue to prefer to trade their securities in the OTC market.

NASDAQ. Prior to 1971, OTC quotations were compiled daily by the National Quotations Bureau (a private company), which published this data on what are commonly called "pink sheets." A major problem with this approach was the difficulty in getting current quotations from dealers. A broker had to contact various dealers to determine which one offered the best price for the investor. This approach was inefficient and time-consuming.

In 1971, the NASDQ started providing automated quotations through its National Association of Securities Dealers Automatic Quotations (NASDAQ) system. This computerized communication network provides current bid and asked prices on over 5600 securities. Through a computer terminal, a broker can instantly see the bid and asked quotations of all dealers making a market in a stock. The broker can then contact the dealer offering the best price and negotiate a trade directly.

Reading OTC quotes. Two lists of NASDAQ securities are published in newspapers. The principal list is called NASDAQ National Market Issues, which includes more than half of the stocks in the NASDAQ system with inclusion based upon a company's financial performance and investor interest in the stock. The list of National Market Issues (Exhibit 1) shows actual transaction prices, like those shown for exchange-traded issues. The information presented is in the same form as that presented for NYSE and AMEX issues.

EXHIBIT 1
NASDAQ National Market Issues

	52 weeks Hi	52 weeks Lo	Stock	Sym	Div	Yld %	PE	Vol 100s	Hi	Lo	Close	Net Chg
S	18¾	13½	Hach	HACH	.16	1.1	19	14	16	15	15	...
	9¼	5⅞	Hadco	HDCO		...	9	270	6⅛	6	6⅛	-⅛
	40½	16¼	HaggarCp	HGGR	.20	.7	10	104	29¾	29	29	-½
	16½	10	HahnAutomtve	HAHN		...	16	230	15½	15	15¼	+⅛
n	12¾	9¾	HallmarkCap	HALL		...	...	30	12½	12¼	12¼	-¼
	21½	8½	HalmkHlthcr A	HMHC		...	15	241	20	19½	19⅞	-⅛
	4¼	1¾	HallwdConsol	HCRC		...	30	9	2⅛	2⅛	2⅛	-1/16
	9¼	5½	HambrgrHam	HAMB		...	dd	159	6½	6	6¼	...
	35½	16	HamiltonBcp	HFSB		...	...	765	30⅜	29½	30⅛	+⅜
	35½	26¼	HancockHldg	HBHC	.92	3.3	10	1560	29 1/16	28¼	28¼	-½
	8½	6	HandexEnvr	HAND		...	33	37	7½	7¼	7¼	-⅛
n	10½	10	HappinesExp	HAPY		...	...	1087	10¼	10	10	...

The other list covers issues that do not meet all the listing requirements (see Exhibit 2). Many of these smaller companies are eligible for the NASDAQ Small-Cap Issues list. Each listing includes the company name, dividend (if any), volume, closing price, and net change based on the previous close.

EXHIBIT 2
NASDAQ Small-Cap Issues

Issue	Div	Vol 100s	Last	Chg
A&A Fd g		130	5/8	+1/16
ACTV		301	5 1/8	-1/8
ADM Tr		262	7/16	...
AFP		25	9/16	...
AGBag		10	31/32	+1/64
AGP &Co		223	1 7/16	+3/32
ATC Env		46	10 3/8	+1/8
AberRs		2392	9 1/8	-3/16
AcrnVn		228	5/8	-1/8
AcresGm		25	4 1/4	+1/4
AcreG un		6	4 1/4	-1/4
Activisn		28	4 3/8	-3/4
Actrade		2	1 3/4	-1/32
AdapSol		282	2 3/4	...
AdapSl wt		64	7/8	...
Admar		279	1 1/2	-1/4
AdvCre		529	2 1/2	...
AdvDep		1046	5	+1/2
AdvDp wt		1028	11/16	-1/16
AdvEnv		405	9/32	...

NASDAQ has been extremely successful. Its dollar trading volume makes it the third largest secondary securities market in the world, surpassed only by the dollar volume on the NYSE and the Tokyo Stock Exchange. The NASDAQ has a share volume that approximately equals the NYSE volume in a single day.

NASDAQ listing requirements. NASDAQ has minimum requirements that must be met before securities are admitted to the system. These requirements are not as stringent as those of the NYSE or the AMEX. For companies to be listed, they must have $4 million in total assets and $2 million of stockholders' equity. In addition, there must be 100,000 shares outstanding held by at least 300 stockholders, with at least two dealers making a market in the shares. Foreign common stocks have different listing requirements.

5

THE SECURITIES AND EXCHANGE COMMISSION

Prior to the Great Depression of the 1930s, the federal government did little to regulate the securities markets. However, the collapse of the world securities markets fostered widespread criticism of their operation. In an effort to restore confidence in their operation, Congress intervened and established the Securities and Exchange Commission (SEC) to administer federal laws that seek to provide protection for investors.

The overriding purpose of these laws is to ensure the integrity of the securities markets by requiring full and fair disclosure of material facts related to securities offered to the public for sale. In addition, the SEC is empowered to initiate litigation in instances of fraud. The principal laws administered by the SEC are the Securities Act of 1933 and the Securities Exchange Act of 1934.

Securities Act of 1933. The Securities Act of 1933 provides for the regulation of the initial public distribution of a corporation's securities and for full and fair disclosure of relevant information concerning such issues to prospective purchasers.

Various civil and criminal penalties are applicable to those who misrepresent information required to be disclosed under this act. Under the provisions of this act, new issues sold publicly through the mails or in interstate commerce must be registered with the SEC. The SEC has special forms that must be used to disclose such information as:

1. Description of the registrant's properties and business
2. Description of significant provisions of the security to be offered for sale and its relationship to the registrant's other capital securities
3. Information about the management of the registrant
4. Financial statements certified by independent public accountants

After the registration statement is filed, it becomes effective on the twentieth day after filing unless the SEC requires amendments. It is unlawful for the securities to be sold during this period. Registration statements are examined for compliance with applicable statutes and regulations. Moreover, if the SEC discovers that the registration statement is materially misleading, inaccurate, or incomplete, it can prohibit the securities from being sold to the public.

The SEC does not insure investors from losses. Nor does it prevent the sale of securities in risky, poorly managed, or unprofitable companies. Rather, registration with the SEC is designed to provide adequate and accurate disclosure of required material facts about the company and securities it proposes to sell so that investors can make informed decisions.

A portion of the information contained in the registration statement is included in a prospectus that is prepared for public distribution. Every investor must be provided with a prospectus. The prospectus includes audited financial statements, information about the firm's history, list of its large stockholders, and other relevant facts.

Securities Exchange Act of 1934. The 1934 Act provides protection to investors by regulating the trading of securities of publicly held companies in the secondary market. Extensive reporting is required, along with continuous disclosure of company activities through annual, quarterly, and special reports.

Form 10-K is the annual report that must be filed with the SEC within ninety days after the end of the firm's fiscal year. It contains a myriad of financial data in addition to nonfinancial information such as the names of the corporate officers and directors and the extent of their ownership.

Form 10-Q is the quarterly report of operations that must be filed within forty-five days of the close of each of the first three quarters. It contains abbreviated financial and nonfinancial information.

Form 8-K is a report of material events or corporate changes deemed of importance to the shareholders or to the SEC. Filing is required within 15 days of the occurrence of the event.

These forms are available to shareholders or prospective investors upon request. Antifraud provisions call for harsh penalties for misrepresentations made in the various filings required by this act.

6

FEDERAL RESERVE BOARD

Money is often viewed as the force that moves the stock market, yet who controls that money? This role in our economy is filled by the Federal Reserve Board. The Fed is our central bank, the bank that oversees the activities of the nearly 4400 commercial banks that are members of the Federal Reserve System. These member banks accounted for 70% of all commercial bank deposits. With its broad supervisory authority over these banks, the Fed also controls the nation's money supply. Because changes in the money supply are so critical to the determination of interest rates and the state of the economy, the Fed is subject to intense media scrutiny.

Structure of the Fed. At the top of the Fed's organization structure is the Board of Governors located in Washington. The Board consists of seven members appointed by the President of the United States and confirmed by the Senate. All appointments to the Board are for 14-year terms. However, the President designates the chairman and the vice-chairman, who serve four-year terms with redesignation possible as long as their terms as board members have not expired. The chairman occupies an especially powerful position, often cited as being second to that of the President.

Implementation of monetary policy. Monetary policy refers to the Fed's management of the money supply. The principal tools the Fed can use to regulate the money supply are:

1. *Open-Market Operations.* These operations control the money supply and are the most flexible policy instrument. These operations consist of the purchase and sale of government securities on the open market.

The transactions have a direct impact upon bank reserves and are employed continuously during each day as needed.

2. *Discount Window.* Discounting occurs when the Fed lends reserves to member banks. The rate of interest the Fed charges is called the discount rate; it is altered periodically as market conditions change or to complement open market operations. It is primarily of interest as an indication of the Fed's view of the economy and of credit demand.

3. *Reserve Requirements.* Banks are required to maintain reserves against the money they loan. When reserve requirements are increased, the amount of deposits supported by the supply of reserves is reduced and banks have to reduce their loans. This tool is the least flexible and is seldom used.

Creation of money. The money supply is defined as currency in the hands of the public plus transactions accounts in depository institutions and traveler's checks. The Fed and depository institutions are the organizations that determine the money supply. Actually, currency (cash and coins) constitutes only a small percentage of the money supply. The money supply exists predominantly as accounts in banks. Most bills are *primarily* paid with checks or credit cards that are followed by checks. Cash is typically used for small transactions.

How is money created? Very simply, it is created by banks making loans. Assume that a bank makes a loan of $100,000 to a company that promises to repay after one year. The bank credits or increases the amount available in the company's checking account. Money supply increases by $100,000 as a result of this transaction. Subsequent repayment is made by deducting $100,000 from the company's checking account. This action reduces the money supply. The principle is simple: making loans increases the money supply, repaying loans reduces it.

What restricts banks' capacity to make loans and create more money? Obviously, when individuals and companies have balances in their checking accounts, they write checks and withdraw cash from their accounts. So banks must maintain reserves either in the form of vault cash or deposits (checking accounts) with the Fed. The Fed requires that banks maintain reserves equal to a specified percentage of their deposits. Deposits are backed by reserves, while loans are not. The deposits represent a liability of the bank because the depositors can withdraw their money. The expansion or contraction of deposits increases or decreases the money supply.

Money supply and the stock market. The money supply tends to influence the level of stock prices through its effect on interest rates and economic activity. Other things equal, an increase in the rate of growth of the money supply tends to reduce interest rates, making stocks a more attractive investment. On the other hand, a curtailment in the growth rate of the money supply tends to hike interest rates, thus making investment alternatives (such as bonds) more appealing than stocks. Clearly, the actions of the Fed can affect the level of stock prices.

The Fed and inflation. When the Fed believes that inflation is a clear and present danger, it moves to hold down the growth of the money supply and raise interest rates. (See Key 7 for an overview of inflation.) Actions by the Fed that affect interest rates can significantly impact stock prices.

The clout of the Fed was demonstrated anew in early 1994 when it became concerned about the possibility of an overheated economy. On February 4, 1994, the Fed took action to raise short-term interest rates for the first time in five years. This step caused the market to plunge that day by over 96 points.

It followed with another boost on March 22, 1994. Long-term interest rates surged to their highest level in a year. In response, investors dumped stocks out of fear that rates would go even higher and choke the growth of the economy. By April 1, 1994 the market was down by about 9% from its level of two months previously.

7

INFLATION

People often complain about the declining purchasing power of the dollar. Between 1970 and 1994, the general level of prices as measured by the Consumer Price Index has nearly quadrupled. Inflation has become an economic fact of American life, and no reputable forecaster assumes that this condition will change in the future. Inflation causes great concern because it results in the redistribution of wealth when it is not anticipated. For example, inflation tends to benefit borrowers at the expense of lenders whenever inflation rates are underestimated over the life of a loan. If $10,000 is borrowed for one year and the inflation rate for that year is 10%, the dollars of principal repaid at the end of the year have depreciated 10%. The borrower benefits by repaying less real dollars while the lender receives dollars whose purchasing power has declined. Hence, inflation causes the lender to lose.

Inflation can also have a corrosive effect on savings. As prices rise, the value of savings will decline if the rate of inflation exceeds the rate of interest. People on fixed incomes are particularly prone to the deleterious effects of inflation. The pensioner who retired in 1979 on a fixed pension found that the purchasing power of that pension had declined by about 50% as of 1994.

Finally, inflation affects investment returns. As a general proposition, common stock prices increase faster in periods of low inflation than in periods of accelerating inflation.

Measuring inflation. If inflation is defined as a rise in the general level of prices, how is it measured? This problem is easily solved when referring to the price change of one item, but it becomes trickier when dealing with a large number of prices, some of which have risen faster than others. Realistically, price changes for all the goods and services in an economy cannot be computed. Instead, a representative market basket of goods is selected, and the price changes of the market basket over time are computed. This calculation is obtained by using a price index that compares the current cost of the market basket of goods to the cost of those goods in the base year. Hence, the price index is derived as follows:

$$\text{Price Index} = \frac{\text{Current Cost of Market Basket} \times 100}{\text{Cost of Market Basket in Base Year}}$$

One way to gain an appreciation for the effect of inflation is to employ the "rule of 72." This method provides an approximate measure of the number of years required for the price level to double. The number 72 is divided by the annual rate of inflation:

$$\text{Number of years required for prices to double} = \frac{72}{\text{annual rate of inflation}}$$

For example, the price level will double in approximately 14 years if the inflation rate is 5% per year. Similarly, inflation of 10% per year means the price level will double in about seven years. Savers can also use this formula to estimate how long it will take their savings to double.

The Consumer Price Index. The CPI is the most widely cited index in the media. It attempts to measure changes in the prices of goods and services purchased by urban consumers. The Bureau of Labor Statistics computes the index monthly based upon data collected in 85 cities from nearly 25,000 retail stores. The index reflects price changes of approximately 400 goods and services comprising seven broad categories: food, clothing, housing, transportation, medical care, entertainment, and other. The CPI is considered to be the most reliable measure of changes in the cost of living for most American families. For the CPI, prices for 1982–84 represent the base year, which is set at 100. For example, the CPI measured 148.0 in June 1994, meaning the general level of prices as measured by the CPI had increased by 48% in the period from 1982–84 to June 1994.

Inflation and investment returns. Inflation impacts various investments differently. An asset that rises in price as fast or faster than the general level of prices is a good inflation hedge. Common stocks have been a better inflation hedge than bonds or Treasury bills. As a general proposition, research indicates that lower inflation leads to higher returns on stocks and bonds. In the years since 1960, when inflation has been 4% or less, total real returns on stocks have averaged more than 12% annually. However, when inflation ranges from 4% to 7%, the average real rate of return on stocks has dropped to less than 3%. Why is the market adversely affected by high inflation? Investors anticipate that the Fed will tighten its monetary policy, resulting in higher interest rates, a softer economy in the future, and lower corporate profits. Therefore, investors in stock should be cautious when inflation threatens to accelerate.

8

BLUE CHIPS AND OTHER TYPES OF STOCK

Investors frequently describe stocks by categorizing them according to risk and return characteristics. Although these classifications are useful, investors should remember that there are no guarantees in the stock markets. Even the safest of all stocks, blue-chip stocks, can be risky. Bethlehem Steel continues to sell below the high of $60 it reached in the 1950s. No stock is always an excellent holding, and every investment involves risk. Investors should remember that a stock commonly classified as a growth stock may rapidly change to a speculative stock and vice versa. With this caveat in mind, stocks are frequently classified in the following categories: blue-chip stocks, growth stocks, cyclical stocks, defensive stocks, and speculative stocks.

Blue-chip stocks. Blue-chip stocks are shares of common stock in a nationally known company that has a long history of profit growth and dividend payments. Some examples of blue-chip stocks include IBM, General Electric, Sears, and du Pont. Blue-chip stocks tend to be relatively high priced and pay a low dividend relative to their price because investors are willing to pay more for the lower risk associated with owning these stocks. These companies are frequently involved in multiple industries or in different segments of the same industry.

Many investors associate blue-chip stocks with the stocks that comprise the Dow Jones Industrial Average, the well-known market index of 30 industrial companies listed on the New York Stock Exchange. The names of the stocks that comprise this index are listed daily in *The Wall Street Journal.*

Growth stocks. Growth stocks represent ownership in companies that have had, and are expected to continue to have, consistently superior earnings growth. These companies typically provide little dividend income since earnings are largely reinvested to finance future growth. *The Value Line Investment Survey* provides listings of growth stocks (stocks they define as having provided superior growth over the last ten years). Growth stocks are more likely to be found in the over-the-counter market since it is easier for companies to grow rapidly from a smaller base.

Although it is tempting to look for another Microsoft or Intel, investors should be aware of the greater risk in investing in growth stocks. By definition, growth stocks are expected to experience above-average growth. If these expectations are realized, investors can earn superior returns. But if the growth does not materialize, or if the rate slackens, the stock prices can fall dramatically. Examples of prominent growth stocks include Wal-Mart Stores, Compaq Computer, and Home Depot.

Cyclical stocks. Cyclical stocks are stocks in an industry that is very responsive to the business cycle. Their earnings and stock prices can decline dramatically as the economy weakens and correspondingly strengthen as the economy picks up steam. Because their earnings tend to fluctuate more, cyclical stocks usually are riskier and more volatile than blue chip or defensive stocks. Stocks of noncyclical companies such as banks, food, and drugs are not as affected by changes in the business cycle. Among the cyclical industries are auto, steel, copper, aluminum, machinery, and housing.

Defensive stocks. Defensive stocks are stocks in companies that are relatively immune to the ups and downs of the economy. These stocks have continually stable earnings in comparison with other stocks. Their prices tend to fluctuate less than prices of other stocks. These stocks are less risky than cyclical stocks. The stability in their earnings is accounted for by the relatively stable market for their products. Examples of defensive stock groups include tobacco, food, and drugs. Investors should consider these stocks when anticipating market downturns

Speculative stocks. Investments in speculative stocks offer a relatively large chance for a loss and a small chance for a large gain. Of course, a speculative stock is not automatically a bad investment. Usually, there is a small probability of very substantial returns. A sophisticated investor may be willing to assume the greater risk in the hope of generating substantial returns. An investment in an oil exploration stock would be a good example. However, this type of stock should represent only a small proportion of an investor's portfolio—and the investor should have sufficient means so that any loss sustained would not mean financial hardship.

Stocks without a long-term record of profitability are questionable investments at any time. The penny-stock market is an example of a market to be approached with the utmost caution. The North American Securities Administrators Association reports that penny-stock swindles cost investors at least $2 billion a year and are the "number-one threat" to small investors in the United States.

9

STOCK MARKET AVERAGES AND INDEXES

Most people—investors, speculators, and bystanders—get their first idea of how the stock market is doing from the news reports of the Dow Jones averages and the S&P 500 figures. Even though these figures are widely broadcast, very few people know what they actually mean—beyond the simple fact that up is good and down is bad.

Dow Jones Averages. The Dow Jones Industrial Average (DJIA) is the most widely followed stock market average. When the market trend is described, this is the index almost always referred to. The index was first calculated in 1884 by Charles Dow, who added the prices of 11 important stocks and then divided the total by 11. The average was broadened in 1928 to include 30 stocks, and since then companies have been added or dropped. Currently, the 30 corporations represented in the index are large "blue-chip" companies. The divisor has been changed frequently to compensate for stock splits, stock dividends, and other factors and is no longer equal to the number of stocks in the index.

Although the DJIA continues to be the most publicized index, there are now also Dow Jones indexes for 20 transportation-company stocks and 15 utility-company stocks, as well as a composite index of the 65 stocks in the three indexes. The names of the stocks included in the indexes are printed each Monday in *The Wall Street Journal.*

The Dow Jones stock averages are price weighted, meaning that the component stock prices are added and the result is divided by another figure, the divisor. As a result, a high-priced stock has a greater effect on the index than a low-priced stock. A significant fluctuation in the price of one or several of the stocks in the index can distort the average. However, over the long term the DJIA has been an effective indicator of the direction of the overall market.

Dow Jones publishes a series of group indexes covering nine sectors of the economy as well as an overall index. The industry groups currently include about 750 stocks. All industry groups together make up the Dow Jones Equity Market Index, which tracks broad movements of the market. The Dow Jones industry group indexes and the Equity Market Index are market weighted. In a market-weighted average, both the price and number of shares outstanding enter into the computation. Use of this method means that stocks with big market capitalizations influence the indexes most.

Standard & Poor's Indexes. The six indexes compiled by Standard & Poor's Corporation are market weighted:

1. S&P 500 Stock Index (also called the Composite Index).
2. S&P 400 Stock Index (also called the Industrials Index).
3. S&P 20 Transportation Stock Index.
4. S&P Utility Stock Index.
5. S&P 40 Financial Stock Index.
6. S&P 400 Midcap Index.

All these indexes are assigned values of 10 for the base period of 1941–43.

The S&P 500 is the most widely followed barometer of stock market movements after the DJIA. Originally it was computed with a sample of 233, but in 1957 it assumed a sample size of 500 stocks. On a daily basis its movement is more representative of the movement of the stock market as a whole because of its larger sample size and the fact that the index is market weighted. It is made up of 400 industrial, 20 transportation, 40 utility, and 40 financial stocks. The index consists primarily of NYSE listed companies, but it includes some AMEX and OTC stocks.

NYSE Composite Index. The NYSE introduced the NYSE Composite Index in 1966 as a service to investors concerned with general price movements. The index is broad-based in that it reflects the overall price changes of all common stocks listed on the Exchange and measures changes in the aggregate market value of NYSE common stocks. The market value of each stock is obtained by multiplying its price per share by the number of listed shares. The sum of the individual market shares, the aggregate market value, is then expressed relative to a base market of $50—a figure approximating the average price of all common stocks on the base date of December 31, 1965. If the index stands at 250 as of a particular date, that means the average value of all common stock listed on the NYSE on that date is five times as much as it was on December 31, 1965.

The NYSE also computes group indexes for industrials, utilities, transportation, and financial stocks. These indexes are computed in the same manner as the NYSE Composite Index, although a smaller number of issues are included.

American Stock Exchange (AMEX) Market Value Index. The AMEX index is computed similarly to the NYSE Index. It measures the performance of 800 issues on the AMEX. The base value of 50 is based on the close of trading on August 31, 1973, when this index was first introduced.

NASDAQ Indexes. The OTC Index supplied by NASDAQ has become widely followed recently because of increasing interest in OTC stocks. The NASDAQ OTC Composite Index is market weighted and covers more than 5000 OTC stocks as well as several subcategories. NASDAQ also publishes several specialized group indexes covering specific industries.

Wilshire 5000 Equity Index. The Wilshire 5000 Index was first introduced in 1974 to meet the need for an index that reflects the performance of the organized exchanges as well as the OTC markets. This index of 5000 stocks is the broadest index and the most representative of movements in the overall market. It is calculated in the same manner as the S&P 500 and the NYSE Composite indexes. Its base value was at 1404.595 on December 31, 1980. In 1993, its high exceeded 4300, indicating that the stocks in the index had more than tripled in value in 13 years.

10

MUTUAL FUNDS

For those investors who lack the time or expertise to manage an investment portfolio, an excellent investment alternative is to purchase shares in common stock mutual funds. A mutual fund is a pool of commingled funds contributed by many investors and managed by a professional fund manager in exchange for a fee. More than 6000 mutual funds are available to meet a wide range of investment objectives. There are funds that specialize in growth stocks, in small company stocks, in gold stocks, in stocks of firms located in specific regions such as Asia, in industries such as oil or medical, and in dozens of other specific areas.

Advantages. Mutual funds offer several advantages that make them attractive for investors:

1. *Diversification:* A diversified portfolio is very difficult to achieve when funds are limited. A mutual fund offers the investor the opportunity to participate in an investment pool that can contain hundreds of different securities.
2. *Professional management:* Many investors lack the time or expertise to supervise their investments. Mutual funds are managed by professionals who have the training and experience to make judgments about stock selection and timing.
3. *Liquidity:* Funds can be easily traded. Quotes on the current value of funds are readily available in the financial section of most newspapers.
4. *Constant supervision:* Mutual fund managers handle all the details of managing the portfolio. These details include stock transactions, dividends, cash exchanges, rights, and proxy statements. They arrange for dividend payments and update the performance and tax records for each investor.

Types of funds. Two basic types of mutual funds exist: closed-end and open-end. A closed-end fund is an investment company that issues a fixed number of shares. After the shares are issued, the company's shares trade on a stock exchange or in the over-the-counter market. Supply and demand determine share prices, which can be more or less than a share's intrinsic worth (its net asset value). For some reason, most of these stock funds trade for less than their net asset value. Thus, investors who buy shares at a new fund's initial offering price have generally seen the prices of those shares drop—except in rapidly rising markets.

Open-end mutual funds, by far the most popular type of mutual fund, are funds that issue or redeem shares at the net asset value (total assets minus total liabilities divided by the number of shares) of the portfolio. Unlike closed-end funds, the number of shares is not fixed but increases as investors purchase more shares. These shares are not traded on any market and are always bought and sold at the net asset value of the portfolio. Typically, large mutual fund organizations manage families of funds that may include, for example, one or more growth funds, balanced funds, gold funds, money market funds, income funds, U.S. government securities funds, and small company stock funds. Usually an investor may switch from one fund to another within the same family of funds at little or no cost.

Mutual funds can also be divided into load and no-load funds. This distinction is based upon whether they charge investors a fee for buying shares. An investor in a load fund will pay a sales fee or commission, known as a "load," of up to 8.5% of net asset value, deducted from the amount of the investment. Thus, a $10,000 purchase of an 8% load fund means that $800 is deducted as a fee and only $9200 is actually invested.

No-load funds are typically purchased directly from the fund without stockbroker involvement. No initial sales charge is deducted from the investment, so $10,000 invested in a no-load fund means the entire $10,000 is actually invested. The performance of load funds has been compared with the performance of no-load funds, and there is no evidence that load funds perform better than no-load funds. An investor interested in short-term profits should unquestionably avoid high-load funds. Long-term investors should compare the track records of various funds, factoring into the calculation any commissions or other expenses.

Don't confuse whether a fund is load or no-load with the annual operating expenses incurred by funds that are paid by all mutual fund holders. Information about a fund's annual expenses appear near the front of every mutual fund prospectus, the official sales document that must be sent to new investors.

Predicting which funds will perform well is exceedingly difficult. But operating expense data is readily available. If you purchase a fund with low annual expenses, you won't necessarily get good performance; however, at least you have an initial advantage over other investors who buy a similar fund with higher expenses.

A fund's expenses are stated as a percentage of a fund's average assets in any one year. On average, diversified stock funds charge 1.3% annually but the range runs from about 0.3% to 3.0% annually. An expense ratio of greater than 2.0% for a domestic stock fund is excessive.

Objectives of different funds. With about 5000 open-end mutual funds available, investors have a wide variety from which to choose. However, it is extremely important that the objectives of the investor mesh with those of the fund. The Investment Company Act of 1940 requires that mutual funds state their objectives and make this statement available to interested parties. The objective of the fund can only be changed with the agreement of a majority of the shareholders. The following list summarizes the broad objectives of the different types of common stock funds:

1. "Aggressive growth" or "maximum capital appreciation" funds assume the greatest risks in the pursuit of profits. Some of these funds have outstanding long-term records, but investors must be prepared for sharp

declines in net asset value during stock market drops. These funds are more willing to use speculative investment techniques, and may deliberately be less diversified than other funds to maximize the opportunity for capital gains. Only the more risk-oriented investors should participate in these types of funds.

2. "Growth" funds tend to be slightly less risky than "aggressive growth" funds, and their price should, therefore, be somewhat less volatile. These funds usually invest in companies that have exhibited long-term growth rates in earnings. These funds, like "aggressive growth" funds, are not concerned with dividends since they are likely to be small.

3. "Growth and income" funds are likely to invest in larger, stable companies that pay dividends and produce above-average earnings. Funds in this category tend to be less volatile and risky than funds in the first two categories. An investor can instruct the fund manager to automatically reinvest dividends into additional shares.

4. "Balanced funds" include both stocks and bonds so as to reduce risk. Funds with this objective are aimed at investors who are less risk-oriented. The inclusion of bonds in the portfolio should reduce the volatility of these funds as well as increase current income.

5. "International funds" invest primarily in foreign stocks or a mixture of foreign and U.S. stocks. The value of international funds is affected not only by changes in the prices of the foreign securities held but also by the value of the dollar against foreign currencies. An investment in foreign stock can lead to a profit or loss in two ways:
   (a) The price of the stock in its local currency can advance or decline.
   (b) Relative to the U.S. dollar, the value of the foreign currency may rise or fall.

The optimal situation is to have the price of the stock rise in the local currency and the value of the foreign currency rise against the U.S. dollar.

Sources of information. Because mutual funds continue to proliferate, many investors are confused when making a decision as to which one to purchase. Fortunately, there are several publications that regularly publish performance statistics. Both *Business Week* and *Money* publish frequent articles on mutual funds and useful quarterly statistics on performance. In late August of each year *Forbes* publishes a mutual fund survey of the performance records of all funds, including an "honor roll" of outstanding funds based upon such criteria as how they have performed in "up" and "down" markets. *Barron's* also publishes quarterly performance statistics in February, May, August, and November.

In 1993, both *The New York Times* and *The Wall Street Journal* dramatically improved their coverage of mutual funds. These newspapers, along with *Investor's Business Daily,* do an excellent job of providing current prices of mutual funds. They also present performance statistics that enable the investor to compare the different funds.

Recent growth. Millions of Americans, fearful of investing directly in common stock, are investing in common stock indirectly through the purchase of mutual funds. The mutual fund industry has multiplied in size controlling more money than life insurance companies or savings and loan institutions. In 1994, total investment exceeded $2 trillion, up 100% in just three years. In response, the number of funds has grown to more than 6000, a startling increase from the 3100 just four years previously and the less than 600 in 1980. At the end of 1993, about 27% of American households owned a mutual fund, up from only 6% in 1980.

11

BUYING STOCKS

To buy or sell common stock, an investor must act through a registered broker or dealer. Although these firms are closely regulated by the SEC, one still needs to be careful in selecting a brokerage firm and an individual broker or account executive, also known as a registered representative. Good brokers should be both knowledge-able about the market and effective in meeting the needs of their clients. Their duties include careful handling of purchase and sale orders, offering appropriate advice and research material about stocks, monitoring accounts to ensure there are no clerical errors, and taking care to see that money owed to customers is promptly mailed.

No special guidelines are available in selecting a good broker. Check with friends, relatives, and business associates for their recommendations. A banker, lawyer, or accountant might also be a source of good information.

Types of brokers. Traditional, full-service brokers can provide information about the securities of companies that investors are considering. These brokers are members of firms that typically have large research departments that make recommendations and offer advice to their clients. Merrill Lynch, Prudential-Bache, and Dean Witter are representative of large brokerage organizations.

Discount brokers provide fewer extra services to investors but charge lower commissions than full-service brokers. Discount firms usually service investors who do their own research, who know precisely what they want, and who can make their own buy-and-sell decisions. Investors can save between 30% and 70% on their commissions by using a discount broker. Discount brokers simply execute orders, employing salaried order clerks who do not receive commissions. They also provide routine services. Examples of discount brokers include Charles Schwab and Quick & Reilly.

For even lower commissions, investors can choose "deep discount" brokers. These brokers provide no-frills service, but execution of trading orders is generally fast and accurate. They make sense for investors who do their own research.

In 1994, price battles broke out in the deep-discount business. The first shot was fired by National Discount Brokers, which heavily advertised a flat fee of $30 per trade topped by a $3 handling charge. This fee applied to all trades of fewer than 5000 shares of listed stocks. This action forced other deep-discounters to lower their prices. Deep-discounter fees on many trades are 10% to 20% of what you would pay with a full-service broker. Examples of other deep-discount brokers include Brown, Forbes, and Waterhouse.

Using full-service brokers. Investors will pay a full-service broker approximately an extra $.30 per share over the fee of a discount broker. Is the service worth it? To many, the answer has been yes. A full-service broker should be willing to provide you with the information necessary to make informed decisions. Investors should ask for research from the firm's analysts, data on price-earnings ratios, growth rates, insider buying or selling, and institutional ownership of companies. The broker should also provide S&P or *Value Line Investment Survey* reports.

To minimize commissions, investors can make fewer transactions and concentrate on larger amounts of stock. Full-service firms typically charge fees of about 2% on trades above $3000, but on a $2000 trade the fee increases to 3% to 4% of the order, and at $500 it can be as high as 10%.

Opening an account. Opening an account with a brokerage firm is not significantly different from opening a bank account. A prospective investor will have to provide his or her name, address, occupation, social security number, citizenship, an acknowledgment that the customer is of legal age, and a suitable bank or financial reference. If the account is to trade in listed options, additional information is required. Most investors have cash accounts, which means that transactions are settled promptly without credit. Margin accounts are used by those customers who wish to gain leverage through the use of borrowed funds (see Key 32). This type of account should only be used by experienced investors.

Placing the order. When an investor decides to purchase stock, the first step is to contact a broker and ask for a price quote. The quote often consists of two numbers: the bid, or price buyers are currently willing to pay, and the asked, or price at which sellers are willing to sell. This investor has the choice of placing either a "market order," which means he or she will receive the best price available when the order is executed, or a "limit order," which means the trade can be executed only at a specific price. All orders are day orders—they expire at the close of business—unless otherwise indicated. An investor can choose to place a "good until canceled order," which means the order remains in effect on the broker's books until it is executed or canceled.

12

STOCK TABLES

Stock tables summarize trading activity in individual securities. For example, composite results of the previous day's trading in stocks listed on the New York Stock Exchange (NYSE) and on five regional exchanges are found in the New York Stock Exchange Composite Transactions table (see Exhibit 3). This table is typically found in the financial dailies and, sometimes in abbreviated form, in local newspapers. It provides crucial information that should be evaluated before making a decision about buying any stock.

The name of the company issuing the stock is given in the third column. Because of space considerations, abbreviations for company names are used. The majority of the securities listed refer to common stock. Common stock represents the owners' equity interest in a corporation. Common stockholders share in the distribution of dividends according to the proportion of the total stock outstanding that they own. Typically, owners of common stock also have voting power and a residual interest in the assets of the corporation after claims of creditors have been satisfied.

The abbreviation "pf" in the stock tables indicates preferred stock. Preferred stockholders receive a fixed dividend, which must be paid to preferred stockholders before any dividend can be paid to common stockholders. In addition, upon dissolution, the claims of preferred stockholders take precedence over the claims of common stockholders. Preferred stockholders usually do not have voting privileges.

EXHIBIT 3
New York Stock Exchange Composite Transactions Table

	52 weeks Hi	Lo	Stock	Sym	Div	Yld %	PE	Vol 100s	Hi	Lo	Close	Net Chg
					–A–A–A–							
	17⅜	12⅝	AAR	AIR	.48	3.4	24	88	14⅜	14⅛	14¼	+⅛
	23⅝	14⅝	ABM Indus	ABM	.52	2.5	14	14	21	20¾	21	+⅛
	12⅝	10⅛	ACM Gvt Fd	ACG	1.10a	10.7	...	1238	10½	10¼	10¼	-⅛
	10¼	7⅞	ACM OppFd	AOF	.80	9.7	...	166	8¼	8⅛	8¼	...
▼	12¼	9	ACM SecFd	GSF	1.10	12.1	...	2060	9¼	8⅞	9⅛	...
	10⅝	7¾	ACM SpctmFd	SI	.96	12.0	...	547	8	7⅞	8	+⅛
n	15⅛	10½	ACM MgmdInc	ADF	1.46	13.4	...	654	10⅞	10½	10⅞	+⅜
	12⅜	8⅝	ACM MgdIncFd	AMF	1.08a	12.2	...	235	8⅞	8¾	8⅞	...
	9⅜	7⅞	ACM MgdMultFd	MMF	.72	8.9	...	177	8¼	8⅛	8⅛	-⅛
	14½	11⅜	ACM MuniSec	AMU	.90a	7.6	...	39	12	11⅞	11⅞	...
	11⅛	8⅛	ADT	ADT		...	13	2039	10⅜	10	10¼	+⅛
	35	24¾	AFLAC	AFL	.46	1.3	13	379	34½	34⅛	34¼	-¼
	46¼	16¾	AGCO Cp	AG	.04	.1	9	2137	44½	43½	43⅞	-⅝
	60⅜	27½	AGCO pf		1.63	2.8	...	934	59	57⅞	58	...
	24⅛	12¾	Al Labs A	BMD	.18	1.3	40	100	13⅝	13½	13½	...
n	23¼	19¾	AMLI Resdntl	AML	.21p	...	...	82	21⅜	21⅛	21¼	-⅛
▲	73	57	AMP	AMP	1.68	2.3	25	5003	73½	72	73⅜	+1⅝
	72¾	52⅛	AMR	AMR		...	dd	4347	58⅜	57¾	57⅞	+⅛

Abbreviations such as "s" are displayed in some of the entries. These abbreviations are explained in a section labeled "Explanatory Notes" located at the bottom of the newspaper page. For example, "s" denotes that a stock split or stock dividend of 25% or more has occurred in the past 52 weeks. The explanatory notes apply to both NYSE and AMEX issues and NASDAQ over-the-counter securities.

The first column in the table reports the highest price paid for the stock over the last 52 weeks, excluding the previous day's trading. The second column gives the lowest price paid over the last 52 weeks. The four columns on the right give the high, low, and closing price for the day and the net change from the previous day. A ↑ or an H at the extreme left denotes that the price is the highest traded over the last 52 weeks, while a ↓ or L at the extreme left indicates a new low for the previous 52 weeks. Any high or low price will be reflected in the 52-week high or low column (two columns on the left) the next day.

A separate table lists new highs and lows for each day of stocks listed on the NYSE. When the stock market has been performing well, there will be many new highs. When the stock market is in the doldrums, there will be many new lows.

Other valuable information besides prices is reflected in the table. Column 5, labeled "Div," is the annual cash dividend based upon the rate of the last quarterly payout. Extra dividends or stock dividends are indicated by appropriate footnotes. The next column provides the yield percentages, determined by dividing the cash dividend by the closing price of the stock.

The P/E or price-earnings ratio is computed by dividing the latest closing price by the latest available earnings per share (EPS), based upon *primary* EPS (see Key 14) for the most recent four quarters.

The P/E ratio is one of the most widely used measures for evaluating the price of a stock. It cannot be used alone when making decisions, however, for it should be compared with the company's past P/E ratios and with the P/E ratios of similar companies. The P/E ratio is generally an indication of how fast the market expects the company's earnings to grow. The higher the P/E ratio, the greater the potential growth in earnings should be.

Many investors use the P/E ratio of the Dow Jones Industrial Average (DJIA) as a standard of comparison. Thus, if the DJIA has a P/E ratio of 15 and an individual stock has a P/E ratio of 12, earnings are considered to be underpriced when compared to the market. Conversely, a P/E ratio of 20 indicates the stock is overpriced compared to the market. There is always a reason for these differences. These P/E ratios may be justified by the growth prospects and/or risk involved in purchasing the stock.

Investors generally prefer to buy stocks when the P/E ratio is as low as possible. Academic studies show that, on average, low-P/E stocks earn better risk-adjusted rates of return than high-P/E stocks. Since expectations are not as high for low-P/E stocks, they are likely to be less affected by disappointing earnings than high-P/E stocks.

Column 8 gives the number of shares traded in each stock, expressed in hundreds of shares. Thus, 75 means 7500 shares were traded that day. Transactions generally take place in units of 100 shares, commonly called a "round lot." A "z" before the volume figure means that the number represents the exact number of shares traded. Thus, "z75" means 75 shares were traded, not 7500. When the number of shares traded is less than 100, it is referred to as an "odd lot."

The Wall Street Journal has several additional features to its tables. Some of the quotations are boldfaced, which highlights those issues with price changes of 5% or more from their previous closing price. Underlined quotations indicate those stocks with large changes in volume compared with the issue's average trading volume. The underlined quotations are for the 20 largest volume percentage leaders on the NYSE and the NASDAQ system. For the AMEX, the *WSJ* highlights the ten largest volume percentage gainers. Both of these features alert investors to stocks that may be of interest.

13

FUNDAMENTAL ANALYSIS

Fundamental analysis involves an estimate of a security's value, called intrinsic value, by evaluating the basic financial and economic facts about the company that issues the security. Once the intrinsic value is determined, it is compared to the current market price. If the current market price is less than the intrinsic value, a buy recommendation is issued. Alternatively, if the current market price is greater than the intrinsic value, the recommendation would be to sell the security.

This form of analysis is in contrast to technical analysis, which looks at historical trends in stock price movements and other market variables to predict future stock prices (see Key 22). Technical analysts use indicators, charts, and computer programs to track prices and predict future trends. They often look upon the analysis of financial and economic variables as too burdensome and time-consuming to be useful in evaluating security prices.

Intrinsic value. The price at which a security should sell under normal market conditions is its intrinsic value. This price is determined by evaluating such factors as net assets (assets minus liabilities), earnings, dividends, prospects of future earnings and dividends (or risk), industry trends, and management capability. Critical to fundamental analysis is the evaluation of earnings, particularly future earnings. Most fundamental analysts cite the expectation of future earnings as the single most important variable affecting security prices.

The analysis of earnings is not a simple task. Fundamental analysts cannot use reported earnings alone as a guide to future earnings. Reported earnings are computed by accountants based upon certain prescribed rules known as generally accepted accounting principles, or GAAP. Earnings are affected by judgmental decisions such as determination of depreciation expense and cost of goods sold. Calculations ignore increments in the market value of assets—a property bought in 1970 for $1 million might be worth $20 million in 1995—and fail to take into account the omission of certain assets and liabilities from the financial statements.

Fundamental analysts must estimate "true" or "economic" earnings. This measure of earnings measures the change in wealth of an entity. Economic earnings frequently differ by more than 20% from the earnings reported by accountants. If developed properly, economic earnings should be a better measure of the capacity of the firm to pay future dividends and generate future earnings.

The evaluation of earnings typically involves the appraisal of four earnings factors:

1. level of economic earnings as well as reported earnings
2. current and future dividends
3. expectation of future earnings
4. predictability of future earnings and dividends

Earnings that are predictable are more highly valued by fundamental analysts than earnings that cannot be accurately forecast. Similarly, earnings that follow a steady upward path are more highly valued than volatile earnings with the same overall upward trend.

Intrinsic value will change as factors that affect stock prices (e.g., earnings, dividends) change. Likewise, stock prices will change as the economic prospects of the firm or its industry change. However, stock prices will fluctuate about the intrinsic value if it is accurately estimated. Factors external to the company, such as general pessimism or optimism, may cause temporary gaps between the intrinsic value and actual price of a security. Fundamental analysts believe that they can exploit these gaps.

Keep it simple. Peter Lynch, formerly a portfolio manager of Fidelity Magellan Fund, largest of all mutual funds, wrote a book called *One Up on Wall Street,* which has become a classic. His thesis is that the individual investor actually has key advantages over professional investors. Institutional investors are at a disadvantage for two reasons:

1. They have to waste time justifying their decisions to their bosses. As a result, they tend to follow the herd.
2. A stock is not attractive until several large institutions recognize it and several respected analysts start following it. As a result, professional investors jump in after a stock has had a run-up in price.

Lynch states that the average person is exposed to interesting local companies and products years before the professional. Investors who keep their eyes open at work, at the shopping mall, and on the road can uncover interesting "stories" to exploit. Lynch offers sage advice to the average investor. For example, he recommends investing only in firms whose products and services are easily understandable. And, he recommends, once purchased, a stock should be held for as long as the story that drew an investor to it in the first place is still valid.

14

EARNINGS PER SHARE

Earnings per share (EPS) is probably the most publicized and relied-upon financial statistic. Because of its importance, investors should know how EPS is computed as well as its usefulness and its limitations. Many investors rely on EPS as a measure of performance without realizing its inherent dangers.

EPS has been called a summary indicator because it communicates substantial information about a company's performance or financial position in a single value. Many financial statement users focus upon summary indicators in response to the increasing difficulty in comprehending financial statements. The accounting rules governing the presentation and content of financial statements are often arbitrary and complex, so that users are bewildered in attempting to grasp their significance. Many investors focus particularly upon EPS because they believe it provides critical information about stock prices and future dividends. However, overreliance on EPS can have several pitfalls. Misleading inferences can be drawn if the calculations that derive EPS on the income statement are ignored. Further, an analysis of the entity's total operations and financial condition requires more information than can be garnered by examining only EPS.

Calculation of EPS. EPS is calculated by dividing total earnings by the number of shares outstanding. (The term "earnings" is synonymous with "net income" and "net profit" to accountants who compute EPS.) EPS is reported at the end of the income statement; it is the proverbial bottom line.

The term "earnings per share" means the net income or earnings remaining for common stockholders after taxes and other deductions. For example, net income is reduced by the dividends due to the preferred stockholders:

$$\frac{\begin{array}{c}\text{Net Income} - \text{Preferred Dividends} \\ = \text{Net Income Available to} \\ \text{Common Shareholders}\end{array}}{\begin{array}{c}\text{Average Number of Common} \\ \text{Shares Outstanding}\end{array}} = \text{EPS}$$

However, the aforementioned simple computation of EPS is inadequate when companies have convertible securities, stock options, warrants, or other financial instruments that can be exchanged for or converted to common shares. These securities allow investors to convert their holdings into common stock at some future time. The presence of these securities means that there is a potential increase in the number of common shares outstanding. In the computation of EPS, an increase in the number of shares outstanding results in a reduction (or dilution) of EPS. A doubling of shares, for instance, results in a 50% reduction. If companies possess a complex capital structure, a dual presentation of EPS is required. Accountants refer to these EPS figures as "primary earnings per share" and "fully diluted earnings per share."

Companies are required to separate securities that could cause dilution into two categories: (1) common stock equivalents and (2) other sources of dilution. Common stock equivalents are securities whose value is strongly influenced by their being exchangeable for or convertible into common stock. The complex rules for identifying common stock equivalents are beyond the scope of this book. Suffice it to say here that primary EPS is calculated as if common stock equivalents that dilute EPS had been converted. Fully diluted EPS assumes conversion of all potentially dilutive securities, demonstrating the maximum possible dilution. Where large amounts of convertible securities are present, the assumption of full dilution can significantly reduce EPS.

Conclusion. EPS is viewed by investors as an important indicator of future stock prices and dividends. As a result, it is widely reported in the financial press. Corporations are required to report EPS to their stockholders every three months. Reported earnings can have at least a short-term impact on the price of a stock, particularly when the figure differs from expectations.

Investors must be careful not to rely too heavily on EPS. Details in the income statement, such as trends in gross margin, may be more important than EPS. In addition, EPS may reveal little about the financial condition and cash flows of the firm. It is one of the many pieces of information presented in financial statements that affect the value of securities and the measurement of management's performance. EPS is more valuable as a guide to evaluating a single firm's performance over time.

Since EPS is affected by the choices of accounting methods and one firm's choices may be quite different from those of another firm, comparisons of EPS between firms should be made with caution. In such a case, differences in EPS may be determined more by accounting conventions and rules than by economic substance.

15

P/E RATIOS

Is a stock cheap? Is the market as a whole undervalued or overvalued? One of the most widely used tools to make this assessment is the price-earnings (P/E) ratio. A P/E ratio simply is a stock's price divided by the company's earnings per share over the most recent four quarters. A high P/E ratio indicates that the market expects exceptional earnings growth, and a low P/E ratio suggests that the market anticipates low earnings growth. The P/E ratio for each stock is listed in the daily stock tables of most major newspapers. Generally, the higher the P/E ratio, the more bullish investors are about a firm's prospects (though abnormally high P/Es of 50 or more usually indicate that the company has taken a one-time charge to earnings, skewing the ratio).

The P/E ratio of any stock that is fairly priced should approximately equal the growth rate of earnings. If the P/E of McDonald's is 15, an investor would expect the company's earnings to be growing at about 15% a year. A P/E ratio that is half the growth rate is generally regarded as very positive, whereas a P/E ratio that is twice the growth rate is usually an unattractive prospect. If you are considering the purchase of a particular stock, it is useful to know what you are paying for the earnings compared to what others have paid in the past. The information about earnings growth and P/E histories can be obtained in the *Value Line Investment Survey,* which is available in most large libraries or from your broker. In addition, many libraries have books published by Standard & Poor's, Moody's, and other financial services that track the earnings records of NYSE, AMEX, and OTC companies.

Stocks with high P/Es implying high expected future earnings growth can be risky investments. These P/E stocks experience sharp price drops if earnings don't materialize as expected. Stocks with low P/Es may be less risky because the market has a lower expectation of future earnings growth. Of course, in some of these stocks the earnings trend is downward, carrying the possibility that the price trend will follow that same direction.

P/E of the market. The stock market as a whole has its own collective P/E ratio, which is a good indicator of whether that market is overvalued or undervalued. During the past 50 years the P/E ratio of Standard & Poor's (S&P) 500 stock index has ranged between 7 to 25. In August 1987, shortly before the crash of October 1987, the S&P 500 stock index traded at a P/E ratio of 21 based on the previous four quarters' earnings. The market's overall P/E had doubled from 1982 to 1987. This increase meant that investors were willing to pay twice as much as what they paid in 1982 for corporate earnings—a definite negative sign. Investors should be cautious when the P/E ratio of the S&P 500 exceeds 18. A buying opportunity is often signaled when the ratio falls below 12.

Interest rates have a significant effect on the market P/E ratio, since investors find stocks more attractive when interest rates are low and bond prices are high. Conversely, higher rates make bonds more attractive, so that investors shift money from stocks to fixed-income securities. Aside from interest rates, a herd mentality periodically grips the market, driving P/E ratios abnormally high or low. Investors should periodically monitor the P/E ratio of the S&P 500 index, which is reported on a weekly basis in *Barron's* and *The Wall Street Journal* and daily in *Investor's Business Daily.*

16

INCOME STATEMENT

The income statement reports revenues and expenses incurred over a specific time period. It provides very useful information as to the performance of a firm for a given time span. (Investors should remember that, *in the long run,* there is a strong correlation between earnings growth and the performance of the stock.) After all expenses are subtracted from all revenues, the remainder is net income, or the "bottom line." The terms income, earnings, and profits are often used interchangeably by accountants. The profit (or loss) is shown at the bottom of the income statement, both as a lump-sum figure and as a per-share amount.

Why is the income statement so important? The primary reason is that it provides investors, creditors, and others with information to predict the amount, timing, and uncertainty of future cash flows. Accurate prediction of future cash flows permits the assessment of the economic value of the firm, the probability of loan repayment, and the likelihood of dividend payout.

Financial ratios. Although there are many financial ratios used by analysts, some of the most prominent ones are based on amounts reported in the income statement. The most widely publicized of all financial ratios is earnings per share (see Key 14). Other important ratios using income statement values are:

- *Gross profit margin.* This ratio is computed by dividing gross profit by net sales for the period. The equation for this relationship is:

$$\text{Profit margin on sales} = \frac{\text{Gross profit}}{\text{Net sales}}$$

This ratio measures the ability of the company to control inventory costs and to absorb price increases through sales to customers.

- *Return on common stock.* This measure is the ultimate measure of operating success to owners. It is calculated by dividing net income by the equity of common stockholders. In equation form:

$$\begin{matrix} \text{Rate of return} \\ \text{on common} \\ \text{stock equity} \end{matrix} = \frac{\text{Net income} - \text{preferred dividends}}{\text{Common stockholders' equity}}$$

To obtain common stockholders' equity, it is necessary to subtract from total stockholders' equity the stockholders' equity that pertains to preferred stock.

- *Price/Earnings ratio.* The price/earnings (P/E) ratio is widely used by analysts in discussing the investment possibilities of different stocks. It is computed by dividing the market price of the stock by the earnings per share (EPS):

$$\text{P/E ratio} = \frac{\text{Market price of stock}}{\text{Earnings per share}}$$

High P/E stocks are usually characterized by greater growth potential than low P/E stocks.

- *Payout ratio.* The payout ratio is the ratio of cash dividends to net income.

$$\text{Payout ratio} = \frac{\text{Dividends per share}}{\text{Earnings per share}}$$

Many investors select securities with a fairly substantial payout ratio. However, others are more concerned with appreciation in the price of the stock. High growth companies tend to be characterized by low payout ratios because they reinvest most of their earnings.

Investors should not use ratios in isolation. Rather, they should be considered relative to the ratios of other firms in the industry or to the relative performance of a single firm over time.

17

CASH FLOW

The newest of the financial statements required by accounting standards is the statement of cash flows. This statement is required along with the income statement and balance sheet. The adoption of this statement was spurred by the dissatisfaction of many investors with reported earnings as a measure of a firm's performance. One of the problems with reported earnings is that the final figure is affected by the accounting methods used and may not be indicative of the underlying cash flows.

Purpose of the statement. The primary purpose of the statement of cash' flows is to report information about a company's cash receipts and cash payments during a period. It is useful because it provides information about (1) sources of cash during the period; (2) uses of cash during the period; (3) change in cash balance during the period. Although this statement provides information about the current period's cash receipts and cash payments, it cannot be used alone to provide insight into future cash flows. This limitation arises because current cash receipts result from cash payments made in past periods, whereas cash payments made currently frequently have the aim of increasing future cash receipts. As a result, the statement of cash flows must be used with the other financial statements to predict future cash flows.

Classifications. The statement of cash flows is classified into three major categories:

1. *Operating activities,* including the typical daily transactions involving the sale of merchandise and the providing of services to customers. Examples include the cash receipts from the sale of goods or services and cash payments to suppliers for purchases of inventory.

2. *Investing activities,* including lending money and collecting on those loans or acquiring and disposing of productive long-lived assets.
3. *Financial activities,* including obtaining cash from creditors and repaying the amounts borrowed or obtaining capital from owners and providing them with dividends.

Focal number. The cash flow from operating activities is the first and foremost source of a company's cash. These internally generated funds from a company's operating activities basically involve the sale of goods and/or services. If operating cash flow is not the primary source of a company's cash flow, the company could be in trouble. The bigger the contribution of operating cash flow to a company's cash needs, the better.

The SEC requires that the statement of cash flows disclose results for the recent three years. Don't just focus on the most recent year. Look at the trend over the last three years.

Free cash flow. There is increasing use in the financial press of the term "free cash flow." Although there is, as yet, no universal definition of this concept, the most widely used version is as follows:

Free cash flow = Operating cash flow – Capital expenditures

Free cash flow is an extremely important computation for takeover specialists in evaluating different companies. This amount gives raiders the clearest picture of how much cash would be available to meet the debt incurred in an acquisition.

18

BALANCE SHEET

The balance sheet is a financial statement that reveals the financial condition of a company at a particular point in time. It is useful to investors because the relationship among different parts of the statement provides evidence as to a company's financial strength, which in turn can furnish clues to its future performance. The financial statement summarizes what a firm owns (assets) balanced by what a firm owes to outsiders (liabilities) and to owners of the enterprise (owners' equity or stockholders' equity). In equation form, the balance sheet is represented as follows:

$$\text{Assets} = \text{Liabilities} + \text{Stockholders' Equity}$$

By definition, the balance sheet must always balance, meaning assets must always equal liabilities plus stockholders' equity. This relationship is crucial in understanding the balance sheet. For example, if a company has assets of $3 million and liabilities of $1 million, then stockholders' equity will be $2 million. An alternative view of the balance sheet equation is to rearrange liabilities:

$$\text{Assets} - \text{Liabilities} = \text{Stockholders' Equity}$$

This form of the equation reflects the fact that stockholders have a claim to assets only after creditors' claims are satisfied.

Assets. The economic resources expected to provide future benefits to the firm are called assets. A balance sheet is classified so that similar items are grouped together to arrive at significant subtotals. Assets are divided into three categories:

- current assets
- property, plant, and equipment
- intangible assets

Current assets include cash plus other assets expected to be converted into cash within one year. Current assets are the assets used up and replenished continuously in the ongoing operations of the firm. The most prominent current assets are cash, marketable securities, receivables, and inventories.

Property, plant, and equipment includes assets with relatively long lives. Assets within this category, except land, are depreciated over their useful lives. Depreciation is a method of allocating the cost of the asset over its productive life. The total depreciation taken to date is called accumulated depreciation. On the balance sheet, the balance for property, plant, and equipment is always shown after a deduction for accumulated depreciation.

Intangible assets embody valuable rights to the firm even though they have no physical substance. Typical examples are patents, trademarks, franchises, and copyrights. Patents, for example, provide the holder with the exclusive right to use, manufacture, and sell a product or process for a period of 17 years without interference or infringement by others.

Liabilities and stockholders' equity. Liabilities are economic obligations of the firm to outsiders. There are two types:

- current liabilities
- long-term liabilities

Current liabilities are those liabilities usually payable within one year. Long-term liabilities will come due after one year.

Stockholders' equity is the owners' or stockholders' interest in the company. Under this category is included retained earnings, which are the undistributed cumulative net income or loss of the firm, less any dividends distributed. The retained earnings balance provides no indication of the amount of cash a firm possesses. It represents funds the firm has reinvested in its operations as opposed to making distributions to stockholders in the form of dividends.

Limitations of the balance sheet. The balance sheet provides information about the nature of resources owned, the obligations owed to outsiders, and the amounts to which stockholders are entitled. This information is of key importance to the analyst who is trying to make intelligent judgments about the risk associated with investments in the firm and about the probability (and amount) of future cash flows to be generated by the firm. However, anyone examining balance sheets should be aware of their limitations.

For one thing, the balance sheet does not reflect the current market value of assets. Most of those assets are shown at their original cost. The exceptions are receivables, marketable securities, and long-term investments. For example, land acquired in 1940 will appear in the 1995 balance sheet at its original 1940 cost. If its market value is ten times its original cost, this information will not appear in the balance sheet.

In addition, the balance sheet omits items that are of financial value to the business but cannot be recorded objectively. For example, the value of a company's human resources or its brand names is not reflected on the balance sheet because of the difficulty in quantifying these assets.

19

FINANCIAL RATIOS

A financial ratio is computed by dividing one number in the financial statements by another. Many financial ratios can be computed based upon the values on the balance sheet. A few are widely reported in the financial press.

- *Book value per share.* This ratio is the amount each share would be worth if the company were liquidated at the amounts reported in the balance sheet. The formula for its computation is:

$$\text{Book value per share of common stock} = \frac{\text{Common stockholders' equity}}{\text{Outstanding shares}}$$

Common stockholders' equity is computed by taking total stockholders' equity and reducing it by the amount of stockholders' equity attributable to preferred stock. This ratio becomes less relevant if the valuations on the balance sheet do not approximate the current market value of the assets.

- *Current ratio.* This ratio is the most commonly used measure of short-run liquidity. It is computed with the following formula:

$$\text{Current ratio} = \frac{\text{Current assets}}{\text{Current liabilities}}$$

Although both the numerator and denominator are dollar amounts, it is usually expressed as a coverage of "so many times." For example, if current assets are $200,000 and current liabilities are $100,000, the current ratio is "two times." This ratio offers an indication of the firm's ability to pay debts as they become due.

- *Debt ratio.* This value is computed by dividing total liabilities by total assets:

$$\text{Debt ratio} = \frac{\text{Total liabilities}}{\text{Total assets}}$$

This ratio indicates the extent of the firm's financing with debt. The use of debt involves risk because it requires fixed interest payments and eventual repayment of principal. When debt is used successfully, however, it provides benefits to stockholders. When the earnings from use of the resources borrowed exceed the interest and principal repayment, management has successfully employed financial leverage.

To take a simple example, a manufacturer might decide to purchase a high-speed machine that would quadruple a plant's production of widgets, from 100,000 to 400,000 per month. If the machine cost $500,000 and was financed by an 11% loan payable over a period of five years, the monthly cost to the manufacturer before taxes would be $10,871.20. Thus, the extra 300,000 widgets produced each month would have to bring in an extra profit of at least $11,000 per month in order for the machine to be a worthwhile acquisition.

20

DIVIDENDS

Dividends are distributions of earnings to stockholders. Although most commonly in the form of cash or stock, dividends can also consist of property such as merchandise, real estate, or investments. Typically, corporations can only declare dividends out of earnings, although some state laws and corporate agreements permit the declaration of dividends from sources other than earnings. Dividends based on sources other than earnings are sometimes described as liquidating dividends because they are a return of the stockholder's investment rather than profits.

Cash dividends. Cash dividends are the portion of earnings or profits distributed to stockholders in the form of cash. They become a liability of the corporation after the board of directors properly approves or declares their future payment. Cash dividends are usually paid on a quarterly basis shortly after the dividend resolution has been approved by the board. Dividends cannot be paid immediately because the ongoing purchases and sales of the corporation's stock require that a current list of stockholders be prepared. For example, a resolution approved at the April 10 (declaration date) meeting of the board of directors might be declared payable on May 5 (payment date) to all stockholders of record as of April 25 (record date). The period from April 10 to April 25 provides time for any transfers in process to be completed and registered with the transfer agent. Investors owning the stock as of April 25 receive the dividend even if the stock was sold between April 25 and the date of payment, May 5. Therefore, on the day after the record date, the stock trades "ex-dividend"—without the current dividend—and usually falls slightly in price to compensate for the loss.

Payout ratio. The payout ratio is the ratio of cash dividends to net income. It is the portion of net income or earnings that the corporation's board of directors pays out in cash. Although about 60% of the average corporation's earnings are typically paid out in the form of cash dividends, the percentage payout varies widely. Smaller, high-growth companies tend to have low payout ratios because they have a stronger need to reinvest the cash generated from operations in capital facilities to finance future growth. On the other hand, many mature, profitable, lower-growth companies follow the high payout formula.

Dividend yield. The dividend yield percentage is often reported in the stock tables of major newspapers. This number is obtained by dividing the annual cash dividend by the closing price of the stock. The annual cash dividend is based upon the rate of the last regular quarterly payout. If the dividend in the last quarter was $.25 per share, the annual dividend is assumed to be $1.00. This number can be compared with the yield of other stocks and with the interest paid on bonds and other debt instruments.

Stock splits and stock dividends. A stock split is the issuance to stockholders of new shares of stock. For example, a two-for-one split gives each stockholder two new shares for each one of the old shares. A stock dividend is simply a small stock split. For example, if a corporation issues a 5% stock dividend, the owner of 100 shares will receive an additional five shares of stock. Essentially, all that happens with these operations is that the total number of shares outstanding increases, the price per share decreases proportionately, and the total value of the owners' common stock remains unchanged.

If nothing is really to be gained through stock dividends or stock splits, what is a corporation's underlying motivation for such actions? For one thing, an unsupported tradition on Wall Street is that a stock price of between $25 and $50 is most appealing to investors. In addition, stockholders seem to react positively to distributions of additional shares even if the total value of their holdings remains unchanged. The price of the stock seems "cheaper" after the split than before, especially in a company with a rising earnings trend. Stock splits often occur following run-ups in the price of the stock. On the other hand, corporations often issue stock dividends when cash dividends are unaffordable.

Dividends matter. In discussions of investing for maximum return, increases in stock prices get all the attention. The focus is usually on finding a stock that will multiply in value rather than finding one that delivers a steady stream of dividends. But wise investors know the importance of dividends in determining total return. In the long run, almost half the total return on stocks comes from dividends.

Common stock dividends rise as a company's sales and profits grow. A stock with a 5% dividend yield can ultimately turn out to be a better investment than a bond with an 8% yield. If the stock's dividend increases at a 10% rate, it will match the bond's yield in six years and outpace it thereafter.

21

DIVIDEND REINVESTMENT PLANS (DRIPs)

Those investors who wish to buy shares of common stock as cheaply as possible have as an alternative dividend reinvestment plans (DRIPs). Over 900 companies offer DRIPs, and the number continues to increase every year. DRIPs are tailor-made for long-term buy-and-hold investors.

A DRIP involves the automatic reinvestment of shareholder dividends in more shares of the company's stock. The process eliminates the brokerage firm as an intermediary between the individual's desire to buy shares and the company's desire to sell shares. Instead of sending participating investors cash dividends, the company applies those dividends to the purchase of additional shares of stock. Plan members can choose to have all or a portion of their dividends reinvested automatically. You can change your dividend reinvestment instructions at any time. As a participant, you will be able to buy additional stock without calling a broker and without any commissions. About 100 of the companies will even sell you the additional shares at a discount, usually 3% to 5% from its current market price.

Plan mechanics. Dividend reinvestment plans are primarily intended to serve existing shareholders. These plans are initiated by companies for several reasons. Some companies wish to attract more individual long-term investors. Others see this as a way to increase their retail business by encouraging more of their customers to become shareholders.

Some companies administer their own dividend reinvestment plans. Most companies, however, appoint an outside party to serve as the administrator for the plan. The minimum requirement for enlisting in the plan is to typically own only one share. The share has to be registered in your name; owning a share registered in the name of your brokerage house will not suffice. If the shares are in your broker's name, you should ask your broker to transfer your shares to your name.

A company will normally send you a DRIP prospectus or description and an authorization card once you become a registered shareholder. These items can be requested by calling the company and asking for shareholder relations.

You should read the plan prospectus closely. The prospectus will provide information on enrollment procedures, initial investments, reinvestment of cash dividends, withdrawal from the plan, sale of shares, price of shares, and reports to participants.

Costs. The basic plan involves the reinvestment of all dividends of stock registered in your name. Under some plans, you can choose to reinvest only a portion of your dividends. The remainder of the dividends can be directly deposited in your bank account by electronic transfer or sent to you by check.

Many plans allow you to purchase additional shares in addition to reinvesting dividends. For example, Exxon allows you to purchase their stock as frequently as once a week and in increments as small as $50. Because Exxon charges no commission, your full investment goes to the purchase of shares.

The Exxon plan allows you to vary the amounts you invest. This gives you the flexibility to adjust your investment activity to keep pace with your changing investment needs. As do an increasing number of plans, Exxon allows you to establish an Individual Retirement Account (IRA) that invests in Exxon stock.

Many companies do not charge for share purchases from both reinvested dividends and optional cash payments. Other companies might have service fees of about

$5 per transaction. If brokerage commissions are charged for investors who also buy extra shares regularly for cash, they are levied at institutional rates. These rates are considerably lower than an investor would have to pay on his own.

Participants may request the sale of shares by giving written instructions to the administrator. Exxon imposes a $5 administrative charge and a brokerage commission (currently about $.10 a share).

Taxes. The tax status of DRIPs is not one of their advantages. You are subject to taxes whether you receive your dividends in cash or have them reinvested. If you buy at a discount, the value of the discount is also taxable. Further, any brokerage fee paid by the company is considered dividend income and is taxed.

Plan members receive 1099-DIV forms each year from the company defining dividends to be treated as income as reported to the IRS.

Further information. Remember that you don't buy a stock just because it participates in a dividend reinvestment plan. DRIPs are a shareholder bonus on a company with promising long-term growth prospects. They don't make sense for traders who like to anticipate market turns. You can purchase new shares only at certain times, and it may take you at least ten days to sell your shares.

Charles Carlson (219-931-6480) publishes a directory of DRIP plans costing $15.95. The *AAII Journal* published by the American Association of Individual Investors (312-280-0170) publishes an annual list of DRIP plans usually in the June issue. The AAII is an independent not-for-profit organization of almost 200,000 investors that does an excellent job of education and research.

22

TECHNICAL ANALYSIS

Technical analysis is the attempt to predict future stock price movements by analyzing the past sequence of stock prices. Technical analysts dismiss such factors as the monetary and fiscal policy of the government, economic environment, industry trends, and political events as being irrelevant in attempting to predict future stock prices. Their concern is with the historical movement of prices and the forces of supply and demand that affect those prices.

Technicians place very little faith in accounting data, citing such weaknesses as the lack of comparability of financial reports because of alternative acceptable methods of accounting and the use of original cost to value assets on the balance sheet. Furthermore, they say that the time it takes to process and evaluate accounting data is much too long. Technical analysis leads to much quicker decisions.

Techniques. Technical analysts use a wide variety of methods as they attempt to predict future prices. Many rely on charts and look for particular configurations that are supposed to have predictive value. Entire books have been devoted to interpreting charts. Some analysts focus upon the measurement of investor psychology, whereas others monitor the activities of mutual funds or sophisticated investors.

The tools and techniques of technical analysis are endlessly varied. However, technical analysts tend to agree on the following underlying principles:

1. Market value is entirely determined by the interaction of demand and supply.

2. Both rational and irrational factors govern demand and supply.
3. Stock prices generally tend to move in trends that persist for significant periods of time.
4. Changes in trends are caused by the shifts in demand and supply.
5. Chart patterns often tend to recur, and these recurring patterns can be used to forecast future prices.
6. Shifts in demand and supply can be detected in charts of market prices.

Compared to fundamental analysis. Technical analysis is frequently contrasted with fundamental analysis, which attempts to measure the intrinsic value of a security by analyzing such factors as sales, assets, earnings, products or services, markets, and management. If the intrinsic value is less than market price, fundamental analysts recommend sale. Alternatively, if the intrinsic value is greater than the market price, those analysts recommend purchase.

Fundamental analysis places considerable reliance upon financial statements, which technical analysts usually ignore. Most technical analysts believe that attempts to measure intrinsic value are futile as well as time-consuming. Technicians don't need to look for new information because that information is reflected in price movements. Changes in demand and supply are quickly reflected in prices.

Because price trends tend to persist, the key to investment success is to detect such trends early enough to benefit from the movement of prices. Technical analysts claim that fundamental analysts are tardy in exploiting trends in prices because of the time they have to spend in seeking, processing, and evaluating new financial information.

Technical indicators. There are numerous technical rules and techniques used to predict prices. Technical analysis can frequently be an arcane art so that evaluating some of the tools is nearly impossible because the interpretation is so subjective. This section discusses several of the techniques that are widely publicized and can be interpreted objectively.

Barron's Confidence Index. This index is published weekly in *Barron's,* published by Dow Jones & Co. It shows the ratio of *Barron's* average yield on ten top-grade corporate bonds to the yield on the Dow Jones Average of 30 bonds. This ratio measures the difference in yield spread between highest grade bonds and a larger sample of bonds. The ratio should never exceed 100, since the yield on the highest grade bonds should be lower than the yield on a broader based group of bonds. Typically the ratio varies from the mid-80s to the mid-90s. Technical analysts regard the lower number as being bullish (optimistic) and the higher number as bearish (pessimistic).

The reasoning behind this ratio is that confident investors will invest more of their funds in lower quality bonds to increase their yield. The increased demand for lower quality bonds will then reduce the corresponding yield.

Because the denominator of the ratio is reduced, the index itself will increase, indicating that investors are confident. Conversely, when pessimism prevails, investors avoid lower quality bonds and increase their investments in high-grade bonds, thus cutting high-grade yields. A reduction in the numerator of the ratio reduces the index and indicates that investors are pessimistic.

Advances versus declines. This figure is a measure of the number of securities that have advanced each day and the number of securities that have declined. Many newspapers publish the number of advances and declines each day on the various markets. The ratio of advances to declines provides a better indication of the trend of the overall market than an index like the Dow Jones Industrial Average (DJIA), which is composed of only 30 stocks, or even the S&P 500.

The breadth of the market is considered particularly important at peaks and troughs. Technicians believe that the market may be near its peak if the DJIA is increasing while the ratio of advances to declines is decreasing. The market may be nearing a trough when the DJIA is declining and the ratio of advances to declines is increasing.

Moving-average analysis. According to technicians, this analysis provides a way of detecting trends in stock prices. A moving average is periodically computed by dropping the earliest number and adding in the most recent number. For example, a 200-day moving average is calculated by adding the most recent day's price to the closing prices of the previous 199 days and dividing by 200. The computation of a moving average tends to eliminate the effect of short-term fluctuations and provides a standard against which to compare short-term fluctuations. For example, technicians consider a downward penetration through a moving-average line as signal to sell, particularly when a moving-average price is flattening out. On the other hand, analysts are bullish about a stock when the graph of a moving-average price flattens out and the stock's price rises through the moving average.

Sentiment indicators. There are several indicators that attempt to measure investors' attitudes toward the stock market. Some sentiment indicators measure investors' attitude directly, whereas others track the recommendations of investment advisers. Technical analysts look at this data differently than what might be expected. When investors are extremely bullish, technical analysts regard the market as vulnerable; when investors are very bearish, they regard this as a buying opportunity. Technical analysts justify this belief by noting that investors become more and more bullish as the market rises, until they have used up their cash. With the reduction in cash available to investors, the demand factor slackens and the market has nowhere to go but down. *Investors Intelligence* weekly polls investment advisers and the results are published in both *Barron's* and *Investor's Business Daily*.

The market is regarded as nearing a top when 65% of the investment advisers are bullish. When less than 30% of the advisers are bullish, the market may be approaching a bottom.

Evaluating technical analysis. No technical indicator has proven to be an infallible predictor of future stock prices. There is no sure and easy road to stock market riches. Technical analysis may be useful for some investors. However, other investors should not feel at a disadvantage if they don't use technical analysis in purchasing stocks.

The investors that have been most successful are those who have pursued a sound investment strategy geared to making profits over the long term. For those investors who want to learn more about technical analysis, Martin J. Pring's *Technical Analysis Explained* (McGraw-Hill, 1991) is a useful guide. Newsletters such as the *The Chartist* and *Market Logic* make predictions based upon technical indicators. An invaluable source of data for technical analysis is *Barron's*.

23

INVESTMENT
NEWSLETTERS
AND ADVISERS

On January 6, 1981, a stock market guru named Joseph Granville told his subscribers to "sell everything." On January 7, the Dow Jones Industrial Average dropped 23 points, a substantial sell-off at that time. The next day, January 8, the Dow fell another 15 points. This call established Joe Granville as the most prominent forecaster on Wall Street. However, his reputation for omniscience faded rapidly when he missed the great bull market starting in 1982.

In the late 1980s, Robert Prechter and the Elliott Wave theory became fashionable. On July 7, 1986, Prechter told his subscribers to "sell everything right away." That day the Dow plummeted almost 62 points, a then record one-day drop. He shortly turned bullish predicting the Dow would rise to 3600. His following rapidly diminished after the crash of October 1987 (he predicted a depression for 1990).

Also in the 1980s, Elaine Garzarelli of Shearson Lehman Brothers became the fashionable guru. Her star status was confirmed when she predicted a downturn one week before the crash of 1987—just in time to allow her clients to get out of the market. She also anticipated the strong 1991 stock market. Later, however, her image as a prognosticator was slightly tarnished by the feeble performance of the fund that she managed, which underperformed the S&P 500 in five of the last six years of its life. The fund on July 15, 1994 was folded into another fund and Garzarelli is no longer a mutual fund manager.

More than a million investors subscribe to hundreds of newsletters, paying anywhere from $50 to nearly $1,000 a year for advice that varies widely in quality and usefulness. Many investment newsletters make extravagant claims about their performance and suggest that following their advice will lead to stock market riches. Investors should be leery of that kind of flamboyant claim, which is found in some advertisements. On the other hand, some of the newsletters can be useful in enhancing the performance of investors.

The various services reflect nearly every approach to investing. Many of them make recommendations based upon technical analysis, which attempts to predict future prices based upon the pattern of past prices. Other services employ a fundamental approach—analyzing earnings, cash flow, asset value, and other basic financial data. Services with this basic approach include the three largest:

- *Value Line Investment Survey*
- Standard & Poor's *The Outlook*
- *United Business & Investment Report*

Still other advisory services are more specialized, focusing on small stocks, stock options, stock charts, insider trading, mutual funds, or other particular areas of investment. Newsletter writers do not have to pass an exam or meet qualifications of any kind. Anyone can publish an investment newsletter.

Evaluating newsletters. Most investors don't have the time or the financial resources to evaluate all the newsletters. Fortunately, help is available. Each February, Mark Hulbert publishes *The Hulbert Guide to Financial Newsletters* (703-683-5905), which evaluates the performance of more than 160 investment newsletters. Hulbert describes each service in detail and evaluates the quality and effectiveness of each newsletter's recommendations according to a number of objective criteria. Hulbert also writes a regular column in *Forbes* discussing the newsletter industry.

From year to year, the performance success of newsletters changes. Only a minority have consistently provided superior performance. Some of the newsletters that have had superior long-term performance are the following:

- *Zweig Forecast* (516-223-3800)
- *The Prudent Speculator* (310-587-2410)
- *Growth Stock Outlook* (301-654-5205)
- *Systems & Forecasts* (516-829-6444)
- *The Chartist* (310-596-2385)

An inexpensive way to familiarize yourself with some of the services is to take advantage of the sample offer made by Select Information Exchange (212-247-7123), which provides trial subscriptions to 20 services in its catalog for $11.95.

24

OTHER SOURCES OF INFORMATION

The purpose of this key is to describe the primary sources of information available to assist investors in making decisions. An investor doesn't need to read all the sources to make informed choices. However, it is necessary to be aware of trends in the economy and business activity. Most successful investors have a broad knowledge of the business and investment environment, so that they are capable of making judgments independent of the so-called experts. Such knowledge is important because the opinions of experts are frequently contradictory.

The most accessible source of information for nearly all investors is the financial pages of newspapers. Newspapers vary in their coverage of financial developments from excellent to poor. Both *The New York Times* and *USA Today* have excellent financial sections. Many investors have also chosen to supplement their local newspapers with a specialized financial newspaper such as *The Wall Street Journal,* by far the most widely read daily financial newspaper. *Investor's Business Daily* is also useful, particularly to those investors who use technical analysis.

There are also many general business periodicals and financial magazines available. *Business Week, Fortune,* and *Forbes* are three major business magazines. *Business Week* is more oriented towards news reporting than the other two periodicals. In contrast, *Forbes* and *Fortune* (both published biweekly) focus on specific companies and business personalities. Investors should examine these periodicals and subscribe to at least one that appears most useful in enhancing their understanding of the securities markets. *Barron's,* the weekly sister publication of *The Wall Street Journal,* provides a wealth of useful financial data as well as columns and features on events significant to investors. *Money* carries many articles on investments and is also a useful source of information on all aspects of financial planning.

Statistical services. Standard & Poor's and Moody's are the two most important firms in the investment information business. They compete with a broad array of products covering the entire investment arena. With respect to stocks, Standard & Poor's publishes a monthly *Stock Guide* and Moody's publishes a monthly *Stock Survey.* Standard & Poor's also publishes the weekly *Outlook* and a series of *Standard Stock Reports,* which are typically available at brokerage firms. These one-page reports provide a useful summary and description of a firm's operations and financial history.

Probably the most comprehensive single advisory service is *The Value Line Investment Survey,* a publication providing a one page summary of useful financial data on individual companies. It also provides separate rankings on a 1–5 scale of timeliness and safety. Timeliness is the probable price performance relative to the market over the next 12 months. Safety is the stock's future price stability and the company's current financial strength. A rank of 1 is the highest. This systematized approach lets the investor know exactly how *Value Line* regards the prospects of each firm. (Descriptions of other advisory services are discussed in the previous key.)

Direct from the company. Before buying a stock in a company, you should obtain all the information you can get from the company itself. You can obtain the phone number of different companies by consulting a company directory at your local library. When calling, ask for shareholder relations. Shareholder relations will send you an annual report, Form 10-Q, and a proxy statement upon request.

The annual report is the formal report issued yearly by a corporation to its shareholders. It includes the president's letter, management's discussion of operations, balance sheet, income statement, statement of cash flows, footnotes, and the audit report.

Form 10-Q is a quarterly update to the annual report. It provides information about outstanding securities, debt compliance arrangements, changes in stockholdings, legal proceedings, and stockholder voting matters (e.g., electing board of directors). It also contains abbreviated financial statement information updating the annual report as to financial position and results of operations.

The proxy statement provides you with information about items to be voted upon at the annual meeting. In addition, it provides you with information about management and directors not available in the other reports to shareholders. Of particular interest is the number of shares owned by officers and directors. This information is important because, in general, the greater their ownership of common stock, the more likely their interests are aligned with those of shareholders.

25

MARKET TIMING

Is this a good time to buy or sell stocks? Stock analysts usually have an answer to this perennial question but individual investors can form their own judgments by looking at several relatively simple yardsticks. The first three indicators involve a fundamental timing approach that examines current stock prices relative to financial variables such as earnings and dividends. A technical timing approach would be based upon stock price patterns. These yardsticks have proven to be effective indicators of the current state of the market. They are less useful as short-term trading signals.

Dividend-yield gauge. This measure evaluates the stock market's temperature by computing the dividend yield of Standard & Poor's 500 stock index. This number is calculated by dividing the aggregate per share dividend of the S&P 500 stocks by the S&P 500 index. Higher dividend yields indicate that cash dividends are high relative to the price of stocks in the index—a signal of undervaluation of stock prices. Lower dividend yields are a sign of overvaluation, since the dividends are low relative to the price of the stocks. Specifically, when the S&P yield falls below 3%, historically, this indicates that the market may be overvalued and investors should be cautious. When the S&P yield rises above 5%, a strong buy signal is indicated. In August of 1987 (two months before the crash of 1987), the S&P dividend yield had fallen to 2.5%—the lowest in over 100 years. This ratio is reported weekly in *Barron's*.

Price-to-earnings gauge. This ratio measures the relationship between the price of common stocks and their annual earnings per share by dividing the price of the common stocks in the S&P 500 index by the earnings per share of the stocks in the 500 index. The market is fairly valued when stock prices reflect reasonable expectations regarding earnings growth. When the price-earnings ratio is high—above 18, say—the market is expecting significant positive future earnings increase—a prediction that may not occur. When price-earnings ratios approach historic lows—under 10—the market may be too pessimistic about future earnings growth. Since 1950, stocks in the Standard & Poor's 500 index have traded an average 14.3 times the previous 12 months' earnings per share. This ratio is provided weekly in *Barron's*. A ratio above 18 historically indicates that the market may be ready for a correction. A ratio below 10 usually signals a buying opportunity. Like all stock market predictors, the P/E gauge does not have a perfect record, especially in the short run. Extreme readings can be reached and maintained for long periods of time.

Rule of 21. This measure offers a simple method of evaluating whether or not the market is vulnerable. According to the rule, when the price-earnings (P/E) ratio of the Dow Jones Industrials plus the current rate of inflation total 21 or more, watch out. Prior to the October 1987 crash, the rate of inflation was 5% and the P/E ratio of the Dow Jones Industrials was 18.4. The P/E ratio of the Dow Jones is available daily in *Investor's Business Daily* and weekly in *Barron's*.

Presidential election cycle. An interesting indicator is based upon the presidential election cycle. Simply put, every four years, stock prices tend to perform much better in the last two years of an administration than in the first two years. This difference arises because the incumbent President in years three and four acts politically to ensure the party's return to power.

Yale Hirsch has extensively researched the cycle, with the results providing evidence of the validity of this indicator (see Exhibit 4). Note that the last two years (election year and pre-election year) of the 41 administrations since 1832 produced a total net market gain of 557%, far in excess of the 74% gain of the first two years of these administrations. Although the evidence is convincing, there have been misleading signals. For example, in 1985 and 1986, when stock prices should have been weak according to the signal, they were up 27% and 17%, respectively.

An update of the presidential election cycle is provided annually in Yale Hirsch's *Stock Trader's Almanac* (The Hirsch Organization, Inc., 184 Central Avenue, Old Tappan, NJ 07675). This publication contains a wealth of information useful to investors.

EXHIBIT 4
Presidential Election Cycle
Stock Market Action Since 1832
Net change from year to year based on average December prices

PRESIDENT ELECTED	4-year cycle beginning	Election Year	Post-Election Year	Mid-term	Pre-Election Year
Jackson (D)	1832	15%	– 3%	10%	2%
Van Buren (D)	1836	– 8	– 8	1	–13
W.H. Harrison (W)**	1840*	5	–14	–13	36
Polk (D)	1844*	8	6	–15	1
Taylor (W)**	1848*	– 4	0	19	– 3
Pierce (D)	1852*	20	–13	–30	1
Buchanan (D)	1856	4	–30	– 7	– 7
Lincoln (R)	1860*	– 4	– 4	43	30
Lincoln (R)**	1864	0	–14	– 3	– 6
Grant (R)	1868	2	– 7	– 4	7
Grant (R)	1872	7	–13	3	– 4
Hayes (R)	1876	–18	–10	6	43
Garfield (R)**	1880	19	3	– 3	– 9
Cleveland (D)	1884*	–19	20	9	– 7
B. Harrison (R)	1888*	– 2	3	–14	18
Cleveland (D)	1892*	1	–20	– 3	1
McKinley (R)	1896*	– 2	13	19	7
McKinley (R)**	1900	14	16	1	–19
T. Roosevelt (R)	1904	25	16	3	–33
Taft (R)	1908	37	14	–12	1
Wilson (D)	1912*	3	–14	– 9	32
Wilson (D)	1916	3	–31	16	13
Harding (R)**	1920*	–24	7	20	– 3
Coolidge (R)	1924	19	23	5	26
Hoover (R)	1928	36	–15	–29	–47
F. Roosevelt (D)	1932*	–18	48	– 2	39
F. Roosevelt (D)	1936	28	–34	13	0
F. Roosevelt (D)	1940	–12	–15	6	21

(continued)

EXHIBIT 4 (continued)
Presidential Election Cycle
Stock Market Action Since 1832
Net change from year to year based on average December prices

PRESIDENT ELECTED	4-year cycle beginning	Election Year	Post-Election Year	Mid-term	Pre-Election Year
F. Roosevelt (D)**	1944	14	33	−10	− 2
Truman (D)	1948	− 2	11	20	15
Eisenhower (R)	1952*	7	− 3	39	23
Eisenhower (R)	1956	4	−13	33	11
Kennedy (D)**	1960*	− 4	27	−13	18
Johnson (D)	1964	13	9	−11	17
Nixon (R)	1968*	12	−14	− 1	10
Nixon (R)***	1972	12	−19	−32	32
Carter (D)	1976*	18	−10	2	11
Reagan (R)	1980*	26	− 7	13	18
Reagan (R)	1984	0	26	20	− 3
Bush (R)	1988	15	26	− 6	18
Clinton (D)	1992*	12			
1904–1992 totals		224%	65%	65%	217%
1832–1992 totals		262%	−10%	84%	295%

*Party in power ousted **Death in office ***Resigned
D—Democrat, W—Whig, R—Republican

Source: Reprinted with permission from *Stock Trader's Almanac* by Yale Hirsch, The Hirsch Organization, Inc., 1994, p. 125.

26

MARKET EFFICIENCY

After the stock market crash of October 19, 1987, when the Dow Jones Industrial Average plunged a record 508 points, articles in *Forbes, Fortune,* and other publications discussed the efficient market hypothesis (EMH) and the insight it offered into reasons for the decline. Although the EMH has been a topic of academic interest and debate for the past 30 years, it has only recently received the attention of the financial press.

Market efficiency is a description of how prices in competitive markets react to new information. An efficient market is one in which prices adjust rapidly to new information and in which current prices fully reflect all publicly available information. Thus, according to EMH, an investor cannot use publicly available information to earn above-average profits (profits that exceed a buy-and-hold strategy). Market prices already reflect public information contained in balance sheets, income statements, dividend declarations, and so forth. According to this theory, then, neither fundamental nor technical analysis can produce investment recommendations that will earn above-average profits (see Keys 13 and 22).

Evidence. Although the EMH provides important lessons for investors, its adherents frequently tend to overstate their case. A couple of points should be emphasized. First, although much empirical evidence supports the EMH, several strategies have been able to beat the market consistently and thus seem to be exceptions to the market's efficiency. A market, rather than being perfectly efficient or inefficient, is more or less efficient. Efficiency is a function of how closely a market is followed. The case for the efficiency of stock prices on the

New York Stock Exchange (NYSE) is undoubtedly stronger than for those in the over-the-counter market because the latter stocks are not monitored to the same extent as stocks listed on the NYSE.

Second, market efficiency varies depending upon the qualifications of investors. For the majority of investors, the market is an efficient mechanism. However, there are investors who consistently generate above-average returns. This performance by a minority of investors should not obscure the fact that all the evidence, including the performance of mutual funds and the recommendations of investment newsletters, indicates that it is very difficult to earn above-average profits on a consistent basis. The EMH is therefore an aggregate concept applying to the majority of investors or the market as a whole.

Lessons of the EMH. Although many analysts are dubious about the EMH, it does provide some important lessons that should be absorbed by all investors:

1. Tips are rarely of value. The market processes new information very quickly.
2. A portfolio should not be churned. A strategy that involves frequent purchases and sales of stocks is likely to be a loser because the commission costs eat up any profits an investor might make.
3. It is not easy to beat the market; only a small minority of investors consistently do so. High returns can usually be achieved only through assuming greater risk. However, greater risk raises the possibility of increased losses as well as gains.

27

MERGERS AND ACQUISITIONS

A merger occurs when one firm absorbs another firm and the latter loses its corporate identity. There are many different ways to effect business combinations. Basically, it involves either a stock acquisition, an asset acquisition, or combination of the two. In a stock acquisition, the acquiring firm obtains controlling interest in the voting stock of the acquired firm and absorbs that firm. In an asset acquisition, the acquiring firm directly purchases the assets of the acquired firm. "Merger" is often combined with "acquisitions" and abbreviated as M&As. When "takeover" is used in the context of M&As, it implies that the acquired firm's management opposed the acquisition.

Tender offer. A tender offer is an offer to all stockholders of a company to purchase a specified number of shares at a specified price within a specified time frame. The offer may come from the company itself or from another company or investor group. A tender offer made to current stockholders by another company or investor group is typically part of a hostile takeover. Usually the offer to buy is open only for a period of up to several weeks. All stockholders have the option to tender any or all shares that they own. The tender offer price is often substantially above the current price to encourage shareholders to tender their shares. The stock price will spurt in response to the tender offer but will settle at a level slightly below the tender offer price. This gap arises because of the possibility that the takeover will fail.

Takeover terminology. Takeover mania has spawned a colorful vocabulary reflected in the financial news. Many of these terms reflect the efforts of companies to fend off corporate raiders.

- *Poison pill.* A tactic that is used by corporations to defend themselves by making unfriendly takeovers more expensive. For example, preferred stock is sometimes issued to give shareholders the right to redeem it at an extravagant premium after a takeover.
- *White knight.* A person or corporation who saves a corporation from a hostile takeover by taking it over on more favorable terms. The white knight is considered more suitable by the target company and is often courted by the target company to make an offer.
- *Golden parachute.* Executives concerned about their positions guarantee themselves lucrative severance pay or stock allowances in the event of a takeover.
- *Greenmail.* Greenmail is a concept similar to blackmail. It refers to a corporation buying a block of stock from a potential acquirer at a price that substantially exceeds the going market price. Management thus pays a premium to take the stock out of the hands of an unfriendly corporate raider.
- *Shark repellent.* A potential takeover target may try to enhance its defenses by the inclusion of corporate bylaws designed to put obstacles in the path of a takeover company.
- *Pacman defense.* The target company attempts to counteract a takeover bid by threatening to take over the acquirer and begins buying its common shares.

Recent pace. Takeover activity was red hot in 1994. M&A announcements through August 2 were up a sizzling 22% from the previous year. The value of the deals jumped even more—$170 billion versus $114 billion, a 45% gain.

This pace hasn't been seen since 1988 when there were over 6300 mergers totaling a record $335 billion. Why is the takeover pot boiling? Companies want to add to market share or cut costs by selling a division or buying up a competitor. In addition, low interest rates and restrained economic growth lead companies to seek acquisitions as a way to grow. Finally, the relatively modest interest rates and the willingness of banks to lend has made the deals easier to finance.

28

FINANCIAL LEVERAGE

Financial leverage is the use of debt to magnify returns. Speculators attempt to multiply returns by supplementing their own funds with borrowed funds. A margin account can be established to use leverage to invest in securities. Under current rules, the initial requirement for margin on stocks is 50%. Therefore, to purchase $20,000 worth of securities an investor must put up $10,000 in cash. The remainder can be borrowed from a brokerage firm. Of course, leverage is a two-way street in that it magnifies losses as well as gains.

Business firms use leverage to increase their income. Like individuals, they use debt to increase the resources available to generate future profits. Leveraging is successful as long as the money borrowed produces returns greater than the interest charges on the additional debt incurred. However, debt involves risk because the firm commits itself to making fixed interest payments. A firm that does not meet its interest payments generally becomes insolvent. Financial leverage is illustrated with the following example:

Assume ABC Corporation has $1,000,000 in total assets, and the firm's capital structure (liabilities plus stockholders' equity) consists of 60% debt and 40% equity:

Assets	$ 1,000,000
Liabilities	$ 600,000
Stockholders' Equity	$ 400,000

Assume the cost of debt is 10% and the firm has an average tax rate of 40%. If ABC Corporation earns $200,000 in income, the return on stockholders' equity is 21%:

Operating income	$200,000
Interest expense	60,000
Income before tax	140,000
Income tax expense	56,000
Net income	$ 84,000

$$\frac{\text{Net income}}{\text{Stockholders' equity}} = \frac{\$ 84,000}{\$400,000} = 21\%$$

If ABC Corporation increases net income by 20% to $240,000, the return on stockholders' equity increases from 21% to 27%, a 29% increase:

Operating income	$240,000
Interest expense	60,000
Income before tax	180,000
Income tax expense	72,000
Net income	$108,000

$$\frac{\text{Net income}}{\text{Stockholders' equity}} = \frac{\$108,000}{\$400,000} = 27\%$$

In other words, a 20% increase in income produces a 29% increase in stockholders' equity. In this case, leverage works for the stockholders. Interest is a fixed charge, and the income generated by using debt in excess of the interest charges accrues to the benefit of stockholders.

Conversely, leverage can harm stockholders. Assume that ABC Corporation's income drops by 20% to $160,000 and the return on equity drops from 21% to 15%, a decrease of 29%:

Operating income	$160,000
Interest expense	60,000
Income before tax	100,000
Income tax expense	40,000
Net income	$ 60,000

$$\frac{\text{Net income}}{\text{Stockholders' equity}} = \frac{\$ 60,000}{\$400,000} = 15\%$$

In this case, a 20% decrease reduces the return on stockholder's equity by 29%, illustrating that incurring debt creates opportunities as well as additional risk. Highly leveraged companies can be risky investments, particularly when a downturn in the economy occurs.

29

INVESTMENT BANKING

Investment bankers are firms that specialize in assisting business firms and governments in marketing new security issues (debt or equity) to pay for capital expenditures like buildings and machinery. The term "investment banker" can be misleading, however. For one thing, investment bankers don't accept deposits or make loans, as do other bankers. Nor do they permanently invest their own funds in the securities they issue. Rather, their general function is to purchase new issues of stocks and bonds from corporations and governments and to arrange for the sale of those securities to the investing public. The sale of new securities to raise funds is a primary market transaction. In their early years, investment bankers operated principally in the primary market. More recently, most of their revenues have been derived from trading in the secondary market. After a new issue of securities is sold in the primary market, subsequent trades of the security take place in the secondary market.

Functions of investment bankers. When bringing an issue to the primary market, an investment banker typically provides the client with four basic services:

1. *Advisement:* Initially, the investment banker will serve in an advisory capacity. When a firm decides to raise capital, the investment banker offers advice on the amount of funds to borrow and the available means of raising it. Specifically, the investment banker will assist the issuer in making the determination as to the general characteristics of the issue and the price and timing of the offering. In addition, the investment banker

may assist clients in analyzing mergers, acquisitions, and refinancing operations.

2. *Administration:* After the decision to issue the securities is made, the investment banker helps the client complete the paperwork and satisfy legal requirements. Of primary importance is the registration statement that must be filed with the Securities and Exchange Commission (SEC) before each interstate security offering (see Key 5).

Most of the information contained in the registration statement is also included in the prospectus. This document must be distributed to every investor who is considering purchase of the new security. It contains information about the issuer's financial condition, management, business activities, use of the funds, and a description of the securities to be issued. Many investors have trouble understanding prospectuses because they are written primarily by lawyers to satisfy other lawyers. Thus, it's sometimes necessary to seek professional help in order to get the full meaning of a prospectus.

3. *Risk-bearing:* Investment bankers generally agree to buy all of a corporation's new securities at a certain price. Then they resell these securities in smaller units to individual and institutional investors. This process is referred to as underwriting. The underwriting process involves risk because of the time interval between purchase by the investment banker and sale of the securities to investors. During this interval market conditions may deteriorate, forcing the investment banker to sell the securities at a loss.

If the issuance is too large for a single investment banking firm to handle alone, it can form a temporary partnership with other investment banking firms. Such partnerships are called syndicates. The advantage of a syndicate is that it spreads the risk of loss over all of the investment banking firms in the group.

4. *Distribution:* The distribution service involves the marketing or sale of the securities after they have been purchased from the issuer. Once the syndicate receives the

securities, members are allocated their portion of the securities to sell at a predetermined price. Investment bankers earn income by selling the security at a price that exceeds what they paid for it—this difference is called the "spread." The selling costs for common stock are much greater than those incurred for selling bonds. Bonds are sold in large blocks to a few large institutional investors, whereas common stock is usually sold to large numbers of individual stockholders.

Investment bankers do not confine their activities to the primary market. They also play an important role in the secondary market. As dealers, investment bankers buy and sell securities in which they specialize. Investment bankers are also involved in trading large blocks of securities among institutional investors. Furthermore, they are involved in redistributing large blocks of securities to individuals and institutions through secondary offerings.

30

INITIAL PUBLIC OFFERINGS (IPOs)

Vermont Teddy Bear Company in Shelburne, Vermont makes teddy bears in all shapes and sizes. On November 23, 1993, Vermont Teddy Bear "went public" (the phrase that is used when a private company first offers its shares to the public) in an initial public offering (IPO) at a price of $10 a share. The stock that day quickly ran up to $19. Few small investors were able to buy the stock at the original offering price. Most paid from $16 to $19 during the first two weeks after the offering. It was the institutions and large investors who soaked up the stock at $10. Small investors jumped on the bandwagon at the higher prices. These investors were persuaded by the rising price to expect still greater returns.

They made a big mistake. By March 22, 1994 the stock had dropped to $9.75. Disappointing earnings caused a further decline to $6 on July 29, 1994. It's likely that the professionals had long since sold the stock. The big losers were the small investors who bought in after the initial offering. Many of them had losses of upwards of 60%.

This example is somewhat typical of what happens to small investors who buy IPOs. They are not able to buy in at the initial offering price so they jump in after it is trading and pay a steep premium. Eventually the stock price settles down and the small investor is stuck with little if any return.

The hotter the IPO market the smaller the chance the little investor will be able to participate. In 1993, the IPO market was red-hot as underwriters raised a record $57.5 billion up from $40 billion the year before. These offerings were accompanied by huge first-day run-ups in price Boston Chicken was all over the business pages when on

November 9, 1993 its stock registered a 143% (20 to 48½) gain on its offering date. It subsequently rose to $51 before dropping to $39 by the end of July 1994, a decline of over 20% from its peak.

Wall Street syndicate managers estimate that institutions get to buy about 60% of the typical IPO deal and 80% of the hot deals. In a normal deal individuals might get allocated 25% of the shares, whereas in an exciting offering they might be lucky to get 5% of the shares. After the institutions rake in their shares, there isn't a lot left to divvy up among individuals. Unfortunately, the way the system works is that the easiest offerings for individuals to participate in are those the institutions don't want to touch. These offerings are often of dubious quality.

What has been the long-term performance of IPOs? The answer simply is not good. A study by Joy Ritter, professor of finance at the University of Illinois, found the average return to be only 5% per year. A more recent study by Prudential Securities of 1500 IPOs that came to market in 1991, 1992, and 1993 found that on average an IPO gained 10.9% on its first day of trading. IPOs do reasonably well after the first quarter but after the first year the return actually becomes negative. Robert Natale who edits Standard & Poor's *Emerging & Special Situations* newsletter has long asserted that IPOs underperform the market in the long term, whether in a bull or bear market. He normally recommends that IPOs be held no longer than three months after the offering. For those able to get in at the offering price, he recommends selling the shares quickly and moving your money elsewhere. Although this violates the axiom that most investors should buy for the long term, the IPO market isn't for most small investors.

Why do IPOs underperform after a short time? Several possible answers exist. One reason has to do with SEC regulatory requirements. Company insiders with restricted stock are prohibited from selling their shares until 180 days has elapsed from the offering date. Once the prohibition period has expired, insiders start selling and prices weaken.

Another reason is that underwriters time the sale to coincide with peaks in the market and industry cycles. Thereafter, the company's stock doesn't seem as attractive.

If you are still determined to find another Microsoft, which soared more than twentyfold in value within five years after its initial public offering in 1986, several guidelines can improve your chances.

- Look at the P/E ratio. A common gauge of value is the price of a stock divided by its per-share earnings for the past 12 months. This information is presented in the prospectus that is given to the prospective buyers of the offering. This ratio should be comparable to other firms in the same industry.
- Look for a sustained rate of growth in earnings per share for at least five years, not a mediocre record with one big year preceding the offering.
- Check a company's profit margins before tax and interest. Stable or rising margins are preferable; falling or cyclical margins are a red flag.
- Review the prospectus for any material problems. They are often described in a section labeled "risk factors." Watch for such items as large disputes with the IRS about unpaid taxes, toxic-waste liabilities, or antitrust suits.
- Note the use of the proceeds from the sale. It is positive if the money is going to be used for expansion or to pay off debt. What is suspicious is when the company's main owners are cashing out by reducing their stockholdings.
- Evaluate the quality of the underwriter. Some underwriters have reasonably good long-term records in pricing their IPOs and supporting them in subsequent trading. Others have dumped a lot of losers on the market. Examining an underwriter's recent offerings can be a clue as to the success of a new issue.

31

ARBITRAGE

The law of one price is an economic principle stating that at any given moment, identical goods should sell at identical prices everywhere in the world. A share of General Motors common stock should sell for the same price in the U.S. as in Europe. If these shares don't sell for the same price in both markets, arbitrage actions will occur and the law of one price will prevail. Arbitrage is the simultaneous action of selling the higher priced of the two investments and buying the lower priced (to deliver against the sale), allowing the investor to earn a profit with no risk. The opportunity for arbitrage exists because of inefficiencies or differences in alternative markets for essentially the same asset. The individual exploiting these opportunities is known as an arbitrageur. Hedged or matched transactions differ from a price arbitrage transaction because they involve the simultaneous purchase and sale of similar, but not identical, assets with similar maturities.

Classic arbitrage. Classic arbitrage contributes to a fair, liquid, and efficient marketplace. As described above, the arbitrageur buys commodities or securities that are selling cheaply in one market and resells them in another market where the price is higher. Thus, the prices in all markets would tend to equalize. Classic arbitrage probably originated in international currency markets where, for example, an arbitrageur could buy a British pound that was selling for a lower price in London than in Amsterdam, and then make a profit by simultaneously selling the pound at the higher price.

Risk arbitrage. As international markets of securities and currencies developed, arbitrageurs expanded their activities to include transactions involving some risk. For example, if heavy selling of a currency occurs in New

York, an arbitrageur might buy the currency with the expectation that he could sell it at a higher price in London the next day. This transaction involves risk but it also carries the opportunity to make greater profits than typically occur under classic arbitrage. Theoretically, the marketplace benefits from the arbitrageur's activities because liquidity is added to the market by purchasing the currency when others are unwilling to do so.

Merger arbitrage. Merger arbitrage has become the dominant form of risk arbitrage. When a merger is announced by two companies or a single company announces a bid for another, an arbitrage opportunity is created. Generally, a discrepancy exists between the cash price of the securities involved and the price offered for the target company's stock. This discrepancy exists because of the risk that the deal may not be consummated. Also, a period of several months is usually involved between the time of announcement and transfer of ownership. An arbitrageur analyzes the difference between the offering price and current price, weighs the risks and rewards, and, if warranted, may bid up the price of the acquired company to a value thought to be appropriate. Again, the arbitrageur provides liquidity to the marketplace by buying securities from those investors who do not want the risk of waiting to see if the deal will be completed.

In 1994, with the pace of mergers and acquisitions at its highest level since the glory days of the 1980s, risk arbitrageurs were rolling again. The takeover boom has provided investment opportunities and has made it easier for them to raise money to make trades. Further, the declines in the stock and bond markets in the first half of 1994 attracted renewed interest in arbitrage on the part of large investors.

Surprisingly, there is one door to arbitrage that is open to investors of more modest means. The no-load Merger Fund (800-343-8959) is the only mutual fund dedicated to merger arbitrage, and the minimum investment is $2000.

32

MARGIN TRADING

Trading on margin refers to the use of borrowed funds to supplement the investor's own money. The investor makes only partial payment for the securities and borrows the rest from a broker. Therefore, trading on margin is essentially trading on credit. The use of borrowed funds enables the investor to take a larger position in the stock market. Borrowing money to expand the opportunity for profits is called leverage.

Rules of margin trading. A margin account is simple to open. The investor signs a margin agreement and a securities loan consent form, which gives the broker permission to lend the securities in the investor's account. (See the explanation of short selling in Key 33.)

All securities purchased on margin are held in the name of a broker—the "street name"—instead of the investor's name. However, the investor is the owner of the stock, reaping the profits and enduring the losses. In addition, investors are credited with all dividends received on these shares.

Almost all stocks on the NYSE and AMEX and more than 2000 over-the-counter securities can be traded on margin.

Three sets of rules govern margin trading:

1. The Federal Reserve Board's initial margin requirement as of this writing is 50%. This requirement means that the investor must pay a broker at least $5000 in cash to purchase $10,000 in stock. If securities are deposited instead of cash, 50% of the current market value of the securities deposited may be used as margin.
2. Members of the NYSE are governed by stricter requirements. The NYSE requires a minimum initial equity requirement of cash of $2000 or its equivalent in

securities to open a margin account. Therefore, on a purchase of $3000, the investor must deposit $2000, which is 66⅔% of $3000, rather than the $1500 required by the Fed.

3. In addition, the broker may require higher initial margin than either the Fed's 50% requirement or the NYSE's $2000 start-off minimum.

For example, assume an investor purchased 500 shares of stock at $30 per share. In a regular cash account, the investor would have to pay $15,000 (500 × $30), plus commission. A margin account would generally enable the investor to deposit only 50% of the purchase price, or $7500, plus commission. The broker lends the investor the remaining $7500, on which the investor will be charged interest.

Maintenance of margin. Once a margin account is opened, margin maintenance requirements become effective. The Fed has no regulations regarding margin maintenance, but the NYSE requires equity in the customer's account to be at least 25% of the market value of the securities held in the account. Individual member firms may require that the minimum equity percentage be somewhat higher than 25%.

If the value of an investor's securities drops below the required level, the broker will issue a margin call and the investor will have to provide more cash. Failing to do so generally results in the broker's liquidation of the investor's securities.

Undermargined accounts. An undermargined account is an account with a market value that is below minimum margin requirements. If the value of the investor's securities falls below this level, the investor will receive a margin call and must deposit additional cash or securities. If the investor is unable to make the required deposit in response to the call, the broker will sell sufficient securities from the investor's account to bring the account up to the required level.

For example, assume an investor purchased securities for $10,000 on margin by depositing $5000 in cash. The minimum maintenance requirement is 25%. To determine if the 25% maintenance level is being approached, divide the amount of the debit balance (in this example, $5000) by 3 and add the result to the debit balance. In this case, one-third of $5000 is $1666, that plus the $5000 debit balance equals $6666. If the total value of the investor's stock declines to a point that is less than this amount, the amount is said to be undermargined by the difference.

Special Margin Requirements.

1. The NYSE can set special margin requirements on individual issues that show a combination of volume, price variation, or turnover of unusual dimensions in order to discourage undue speculation.
2. Margin rules now apply to some mutual funds.
3. Stock valued at less than $5 per share usually cannot be purchased on margin.

33

SHORT SALES

Most investors purchase stock with the expectation that a profit will eventually be made from a rise in the price of the stock. However, investors have an alternative way of generating a profit when they believe that a stock is overpriced and expect its price to decline. The strategy adopted in this case is to sell the stock short. A short sale is the sale of a security that is not owned with the intention of purchasing it later at a lower price. The investor borrows the security from another investor through a broker and sells it in the market. (Usually a broker has other clients who own the security, generally in a margin account, and are willing to loan shares; see Key 32).

An important aspect of a short sale order is that an investor does not receive the proceeds of the order at the time the trade is executed. In a short sale, the money is kept by the brokerage firm until the short sale is covered (security purchased). Furthermore, to ensure that the short position will be covered in the event of a rise in the price of the stock, the broker requires the posting of collateral.

A large short position in a stock is not necessarily a bearish or pessimistic indicator, according to many analysts. They theorize that a large pent-up demand exists for the stock by investors who ultimately will have to purchase it to pay back their borrowed stock. In such a case, a sudden buying rush is possible if the stock's price increases and investors cover their shorts and thus limit their losses. A large short interest can therefore be an indicator that a stock's price will be volatile. Short-interest reports on stocks listed on the New York and American stock exchanges, and the NASDAQ over-the-counter market are printed soon after the middle of each month in the financial press.

Technical points. First, a short sale can only be made on an uptick trade. In other words, a sale can occur only after an *increase* of ⅛ of a point or more in the security's price. This restriction was implemented to prevent traders from forcing a profit on a short sale by continually selling short and thus pushing the price down. Second, a short seller is responsible for the dividends to the investor who loaned the stock. The purchaser of the stock sold short receives the dividend from the corporation. As a result, the short seller must pay the same amount to the investor who loaned the stock.

Risk of short selling. Short selling involves the ability to spot an overvalued stock. The price of a stock may seem too high but the problem is that you never know how high the shares you shorted can go. Many short sellers lose money not by being wrong but by being early. A stock's price could go higher and higher, with the short sellers incurring larger and larger losses. When you buy a stock you know that its price cannot go lower than zero. If you short a stock that is going up, the sky is the limit for the losses.

34

INSIDER TRADING

An insider is typically defined as a director, officer, or major stockholder of a corporation. The Securities and Exchange Commission (SEC) requires that the names of insiders be filed with the SEC. Subsequently, they must file reports for any month where there was any change in their holdings. The purpose of this requirement is to enable the SEC and stockholders to observe the actions of insiders and to prevent abuses in the use of insider information to make profits by speculating in their own stocks. These insider reports are made public and are widely reported in the financial press.

Insiders are not prevented from trading in their own securities. Rather, insider trading sanctions are designed to prevent the misuse of confidential information not available to the general public. Some insiders buy and sell securities to make profits through their own accounts; others relay information to others who buy or sell securities before this information is available to the general public.

Insider trading abuses have received wide publicity in recent years. A prominent example is the case of Ivan Boesky, a Wall Street professional investor who was sentenced to prison and fined more than $100 million. He had received confidential information about possible takeovers and other deals from investment bankers. Thus, while not an insider himself, Boesky was able to use illegally obtained inside information to buy shares in a takeover target before other investors.

Corporate insiders who trade their companies' stocks must report all the details of the trade to the SEC on or before the tenth of the month following the trade. For example, an insider trade on January 5 must be reported by February 10. The SEC collects this information and releases it daily at its offices in Washington, D.C. In addition, the transaction reports are published monthly in the SEC Official Summary of Security Transactions and Holdings.

The information can be obtained by writing to:

Official Summary of Security Transactions
  and Holdings
Superintendent of Documents
U.S. Government Printing Office
Washington, D.C. 20402

The cost is $92 for a one-year subscription. This information is also widely reported in the press and is published weekly in *The Wall Street Journal, Barron's,* and *Investor's Business Daily.*

Using insider data. Logically, insiders should have superior knowledge of the real value of their companies. Corporate insiders should be better informed about the company's current business activities and future prospects than either stockholders or security analysts. Although they can't legally purchase stock based on material, nonpublic information, they can purchase stock based upon their perception that the intrinsic worth of the stock exceeds the current market price.

A further legal provision limiting the right of insiders to speculate in the stock of their own companies has significant implications for investors. The rule prohibits insiders from selling shares for a profit unless they have been held for a period of at least six months. Any profit from the purchase or sale of the stock realized within a period of six months can be claimed by the company. This rule requires insiders to be in effect long-term investors.

Although several market forecasters use total insider activity to anticipate broad stock market movements (available in *Barron's* weekly), the relationship between total insider buying and selling and changes in the overall market is rather tenuous. For example, indicators of insider activity would be considered neutral to bullish prior to the crash of October 1987. However, insider data is a very useful clue to the prospects of individual firms. Several academic studies have found that stocks insiders buy outperform the market.

Martin Zweig, a prominent investment adviser, defines an insider-buy signal as indicated when three or more insiders have bought and none have sold a stock within the most recent three-month period. Conversely, he defines an insider-sell signal as indicated when three or more insiders sell and none buy within that same period. These signals are not as accurate in bear markets because insiders may sell stocks for tax or other reasons not related to their perceptions of how well or how poorly their companies are doing.

35

GOLD STOCKS

From 1934 to 1971, the U.S. maintained a policy of buying and selling gold at a fixed price of $35 per ounce. Thus the U.S. dollar was regarded as a substitute for gold and, therefore, as "good as gold." This policy prevailed until the Nixon administration suspended the dollar's convertibility into gold in 1971. There is no longer a link between gold and the international value of the dollar. The value of gold is now determined by market forces. In the 1970s the price of gold zoomed upward and peaked in 1980 at $570 an ounce before falling to a low of $308 in 1984.

Gold had a wild ride in 1993. After hitting a seven-year low of $326 an ounce in March, it zoomed to $407 in July—a three-year high. It finished the year at $391. Gold mining stocks climbed an average of 80% in 1993. In the first half of 1994, gold settled down and was trading for $388 on August 1, 1994.

Traditionally it has been said that an ounce of gold will buy a tailor-made man's suit. Surprisingly, this relationship has held for hundreds of years. Gold has been a remarkably constant source of value through time. For 5000 years, gold has been more of an alternative currency than a commodity and has been used as money. Its universal acceptability has been due to its relative scarcity as well as its glitter. Recently, the world's stock of gold has increased at a rate of 2% per year, from 100,000 tons in 1987 to about 115,000 tons in 1994. National money supplies have increased considerably faster than gold, however, explaining why gold has appreciated more than money.

Although estimates can be made of changes in supply, predicting demand is much more difficult. Over 50% of the gold produced is used for decorative purposes, 20% for official coins, 20% to 25% for industrial uses, and the

101

remainder for private investment holdings. Since only 20% to 25% is designated for industrial use, the demand for gold is highly unpredictable. Gold has become a barometer for confidence in political and currency stability. When inflation heats up, demand for gold increases, pushing its price upward. On the other hand, when prices are relatively stable, gold becomes less attractive. Purchases of gold also surge when political events take a serious turn, whereas a politically stable environment reduces the interest in gold. Finally, high interest rates on money market instruments and securities make them more attractive as investments than gold, which has no yield or interest. All of these factors make forecasting gold prices very difficult.

Gold stocks. A number of Canadian and American gold mining companies are traded on various stock markets around the world. When investors purchase stocks, they are not just buying gold but also a company whose stock is influenced by such factors as management performance, production costs, quality of the ore, and lifetime of the deposit. In addition, many gold stocks pay dividends, unlike other gold investments such as coins and bullion, which do not pay any return during the holding period.

The prices of gold stocks generally tend to closely track changes in the price of gold, although gold stock prices tend to be more volatile than the price of gold bullion because costs of production are relatively fixed. With costs of $200 to $350 per ounce to mine gold, the profitability of mines dramatically increases when prices rise above that amount. Among the better known stocks are: Placer Dome, American Barrick, Echo Bay Mines, Homestake Mining Company, and Newmont Mining.

Gold mutual funds. Gold mutual funds provide several advantages to investors who desire to invest in gold stocks but don't feel comfortable selecting individual stocks. These mutual funds handle the details of stock transactions. In addition, the managers have more time and experience to select from among gold stocks than most individual investors. Finally, they provide the opportunity to invest in a portfolio of gold stocks with limited capital rather than investing in one or two stocks.

The following is a list of selected mutual funds specializing in gold stocks:

- *Fidelity Select Precious Metals*
  800-544-8888
- *Franklin Gold Fund*
  800-342-5236
- *Benham Gold Equities*
  800-321-8321
- *US Gold Shares*
  800-873-8637
- *Vanguard Gold and Precious Metals*
  (800) 662-7447

Is gold a smart investment? Many experts recommend investing 5% to 10% of personal savings in gold. This advice seems reasonable when an investor wishes to diversify holdings or hedge against inflation or economic instability. However, investing a large percentage of assets in gold is not recommended. Although gold prices have trended upward, they are extremely volatile, and sharp drops in prices can and do take place.

36

FOREIGN SECURITIES

As the world economy becomes increasingly interdependent, many investors are now realizing the profits to be made by investing in foreign securities. With about half of the world's publicly traded stocks registered outside the United States, opportunities abound for the investor willing to expend the time and effort in analyzing these markets. Returns on U.S stocks have lagged behind many of these markets. Over the past 24 years (1969–1993), the Morgan Stanley Capital International Index, which reflects all major stock markets outside North America, has gained 904%, more than threefold the 277% increase of the U.S. market.

An investment in a foreign stock can lead to a profit or loss in two ways:

1. The price of the stock in its local currency can advance or decline.
2. Relative to the U.S. dollar, the value of the foreign currency may rise or fall.

The optimal situation is to have the price of the stock rise in the local currency and the value of the foreign currency rise against the U.S. dollar.

Of the several different methods for investing in foreign stock, the two most popular for individual investors are American Depository Receipts (ADRs) and mutual funds.

American Depository Receipts (ADRs). Individuals who wish to purchase specific foreign securities should purchase ADRs, which are negotiable receipts representing ownership of stock in a foreign corporation traded on an exchange. ADRs are only issued on widely held and actively traded corporations. Furthermore, they are very liquid and have transaction costs comparable to U.S. stock. They are issued by an American bank and represent shares on deposit with that bank's foreign office or custodian. ADRs allow investors to buy or sell foreign securities without actually taking physical possession of these securities. Purchase is made in U.S. dollars, and dividends are received in U.S. dollars. Approximately 1200 foreign corporations have ADRs listed against their securities, with the great majority traded in the over-the-counter market.

Mutual funds. The easiest way to invest in foreign securities is to invest in one of the mutual funds that invest in such securities. This course would be preferable for those investors who lack the time or inclination to investigate this market. International stock funds offer the advantage of participation in a diversified portfolio of foreign stock as well as professional management. International funds are now available that specialize in particular regions, such as Asia, or specific countries, such as Brazil or Germany. Prior to purchasing any of these funds, the investor should obtain a copy of the prospectus, which describes the investment philosophy of the fund. Some of the international stock funds that have been particularly good performers include those listed below.

- *Tweedy, Browne Global Value*
  800-221-4268
- *Scudder Global*
  800-225-2470
- *Warburg Pincus International Equity*
  800-257-5614
- *Janus Worldwide*
  800-525-3713
- *T. Rowe Price International*
  800-638-5660

37

CONVERTIBLE SECURITIES

A convertible security is either a convertible bond or a convertible preferred stock that can be exchanged for common stock at a certain price or within a particular time frame. Once it has been exchanged or converted into common stock, the security cannot be converted back. Convertible bonds provide investors with a fixed interest payment. Convertible preferred stock provides investors with a stipulated dividend. The fact that in addition to these payments convertible securities can also be redeemed for the company's common stock, under certain circumstances, means that holders of these securities can reap the benefits of rising stock prices but also be insulated from the effects of falling prices. These defensive investments were offered by nearly 600 companies valued at $108 billion in 1993.

Convertible bonds. Convertible bonds generally have a face or par value of $1000 for each bond. This means that the corporation promises to pay $1000 to the holder at maturity. In addition, the corporation also pays a fixed rate of interest, which typically is less than the interest on a nonconvertible bond because of the value of the conversion feature. Investors are willing to accept a lower rate of interest in return for the opportunity to participate in the appreciation of the common stock.

Convertible preferred stock. Convertible preferred stock is not as prevalent as convertible bonds. Most convertible preferred stock is issued as a result of mergers, in order to provide income to holders of the security without diluting the common stock of the acquiring firm. The rights of preferred shareholders are subordinate to those of bondholders in distributions and in any corporate liq-

106

uidation; however, dividends must be paid on preferred stock before any dividends can be paid to common stockholders. Similar to convertible bonds, such stock provides a fixed dividend while still allowing participation in the appreciation of the price of the common stock through the right of conversion.

Advantages to the investor. Convertible securities combine the safety and fixed income of bonds or preferred stock with the potential for capital appreciation of common stock. Actually, holders of convertible securities don't even have to redeem their securities to participate in rising stock prices. Typically, the price of the convertible security will rise with the price of the stock, although it never rises as much. On the other hand, if the stock price declines, the price of the convertible will also decline, again by not as much. In this case, the interest specified on the convertible bond or the dividend on the convertible preferred stock serves to brake the decline in price.

Many of the companies issuing convertible securities are smaller companies whose common stock is speculative in nature. Typically, many of these companies have a low dividend yield on their common stock, making the common stock an unattractive investment for those investors for whom current return is important. Convertible securities provide these investors with an alternative way to invest in the possible growth of the company while earning a good current return.

As a general rule, convertible securities are callable, which means a company can call in the security and redeem it for cash. Seldom are they ever actually redeemed, however. The purpose of the call provision is to force conversion of the issue when the conversion value of the security is significantly above the call price. If the convertible security is called when the market value of the stock is greater than the conversion value of the bond, conversion is advisable.

Convertible securities are denoted by the initial "w" in the current yield column of the bond tables. Surveys of convertible securities are regularly published in *Moody's Bond Record* and in Standard & Poor's *Bond Guide*.

38

STOCK OPTIONS

Trading volume in stock options has grown remarkably since the creation of the Chicago Board Options Exchange (CBOE) in 1973. The listed option has become a practical investment vehicle for institutions and individuals seeking profit or protection. The CBOE is the world's largest options marketplace and is the nation's second largest securities exchange. Options are also traded on the American Stock Exchange, the New York Stock Exchange, the Pacific Stock Exchange, and the Philadelphia Stock Exchange. Options are written on common stock, securities, and other goods. The CBOE trades options on listed and over-the-counter stocks, Standard & Poor's 100 and 500 market indexes and U.S. Treasury bonds and notes.

What are options? An option is a contract that provides to its holder (buyer) the right to purchase from or sell to the issuer (writer) a specified interest at a designated price called the exercise price (striking price) for a given period of time. Therefore, three conditions are specified in options contracts:

1. the property to be delivered
2. the price of the property
3. a specified time period during which the right held by the buyer can be exercised

Options have standardized terms including the exercise price and the expiration time. This standardization makes it possible for buyers or writers of options to close out their positions by offsetting sales and purchases. By selling an option with the same terms as the one purchased, or buying an option with the same terms as the one sold, an investor can liquidate a position at any time.

Two types of option contracts exist—the *call option* and the *put option*. A call option gives the buyer the right to purchase a specified quantity of the underlying interest at a fixed price at any time during the life of the option. For example, an option to buy 100 shares of the common stock of ABC Corporation is an ABC call option.

Alternatively, a put option gives the buyer the right to sell a specified quantity of the underlying interest at a fixed price at any time during the life of the option. An option to sell 100 shares of common stock of ABC Corporation at a particular price is an ABC put option.

Options nomenclature. Certain terminology is unique to options trading. Some of the more important terms are:

- *Option writer.* The seller or issuer of an option contract. For example, if an ABC call option is exercised by the buyer of the option, the option writer is obligated to deliver the required number of shares of ABC common stock.
- *Option buyer or holder.* The buyer of an option contract. For example, the buyer of an ABC call or put has the right, although not the obligation, to purchase or sell, respectively, shares of ABC Corporation common stock at a specified price within a specified period of time.
- *Exercise or striking price.* The price at which the holder can sell to or buy from the writer the item underlying the option. For example, an ABC 50 call option gives the buyer the right to purchase 100 shares of ABC stock at a price of $50 per share. On the other hand, an ABC 40 put option gives the buyer the right to sell 100 shares of ABC Corporation common stock at a price of $40 per share.
- *Expiration date.* The last date on which the buyer is entitled to exercise an option. However, if an option is not exercised or sold prior to that expiration date, it is worthless.
- *Premium.* The price that the buyer of an option pays (and that the writer of an option receives) for the option. Premiums vary in response to such variables as

the relationship between the exercise price and the current market value of the underlying security, the volatility of the underlying security, the amount of time remaining until the expiration date, current interest rates, and the effect of supply and demand in the options market.

- *Out-of-the-money option.* When the striking price of a call option is higher than the market price of the underlying interest, or when the striking price of the put option is lower than the market value of the underlying interest, it is "out of the money."
- *In-the-money option.* When the striking price of a call option is lower than the market value of the underlying interest, or when the striking price of a put option is higher than the market price of the underlying interest, it is "in the money."

Options versus stock. Options traded on exchanges such as the CBOE are similar in many respects to securities traded on other exchanges:

1. Options are listed securities.
2. Orders to buy or sell options are handled by brokers in the same manner as orders to buy and sell stock. Similarly, orders on listed options are executed on the trading floor of a national exchange where trading is conducted in an auction market.
3. The price, volume, and other information about options are almost instantly available, just as is this information for stock.

Differences between stocks and options are:

1. Unlike shares of common stock, there is no fixed number of options. The number of options depends upon the number of buyers and sellers.
2. Unlike stock, there are no certificates as evidence of ownership. Ownership of options is indicated by printed statements prepared by the involved brokerage firms.
3. An option is a wasting asset. If an option is not sold or exercised prior to the expiration date, it becomes

worthless. The holder therefore loses the full purchase price.

Who should buy options? Options have some definite advantages. First, the maximum loss is limited to the premium paid for the option. Maximum loss exposure is determinable in advance in the event the optioned security moves against expectations. In addition, options can produce quick profits with little capital. Finally, options are flexible and can be combined with other investments to protect positions and make profits.

However, only investors with well-defined investment objectives and a plan for realizing these objectives should trade in options. Successful options traders thoroughly research options, understand options strategies, and closely follow the options market on a day-to-day basis. Explanatory material on options trading is available from the CBOE, LaSalle at Van Buren, Chicago, Illinois 60605 (800-537-4258).

39

FINANCIAL FUTURES

A futures contract is an agreement between seller and buyer, respectively, to deliver and take delivery of a commodity or security at a specified future date. Financial futures are futures contracts written on securities, currency, or various stock indexes. Unlike commodity futures, delivery does not involve a physical commodity. Rather, financial securities or cash are involved in any delivery needed to fulfill the contract.

Financial futures are used by borrowers, lenders, investors, and others to protect their investments by hedging. Institutions and individuals can take positions in the futures market to protect the gains they have made in the cash market. Speculators can also use futures to profit from anticipated changes in interest rates, foreign exchange rates, or movements in the stock market. However, caution is necessary. This market is extremely speculative, and only a small percentage of an investment portfolio should be committed to trading financial futures. As a general rule, small investors should avoid the futures markets. Those who don't generally lose money.

Development of the financial futures market. Commodities futures trading began in the U.S. in the mid-19th century, originally to smooth out the seasonal supply and demand of agricultural products. Since that time these futures have grown into a huge market for speculation and hedging by many different participants. Futures for precious metals, foreign currencies, and other monetary vehicles have since evolved.

The futures market for U.S. Treasury bonds, introduced in 1977, represented the initial market in financial futures. The wide acceptance and use of these instruments led to the introduction of futures representing a wide variety of financial instruments. For example, futures trading includes Treasury bills, bonds, and notes, Ginnie Maes, 90-day certificates of deposit, 90-day Eurodollars, and several stock indexes.

Financial futures are traded on a regulated exchange complete with established rules for the performance of contracts. The exchange clearinghouse acts as a third party and guarantor to all transactions, thus eliminating the need for sellers and buyers to become known to one another. While a future is a commitment to buy or sell at some point in the future, delivery of the underlying instrument rarely occurs. Trades in futures contracts are settled by entering into the offsetting position.

By 1993, no less than 62% of all futures trades in the U.S. were financial futures. Based upon these figures, financial futures appear to be fulfilling an important need.

Arithmetic of financial futures trading. Perhaps more than any other form of speculation or investment, gains and losses in futures trading are highly leveraged. In fact, only a small amount of cash (called margin) is required to buy or sell a futures contract. The smaller the margin in comparison to the value of the futures contract, the greater the leverage. For example, assume that in anticipation of rising stock prices, an investor buys one June S&P 500 stock index futures contract at a time when the June index is trading at 400. Also, assume the initial margin requirement is $6000. Since the value of the futures contract is $500 times the index, each one-point change in the index represents a $500 gain or loss.

An increase in the index from 400 to 412 would double the $6000 margin deposit, and a decrease from 400 to 388 would eliminate it. All it takes is a 3% change in the stock index to produce a 100% gain or loss. Low margin requirements sharply increase the profit or loss potential. A clear understanding of the concept of leverage as well as the amount of gain or loss that will result from any given change in the futures price of the particular futures contract traded is essential for anyone who ventures into this market.

Further information on futures can be obtained from the Chicago Board of Trade, 141 West Jackson Blvd., Chicago, Illinois 60604 (312-435-3500).

Commodity funds. Another way of participating in futures trading is through a commodity pool, which is similar in concept to a common stock mutual fund. Your money is combined with that of other participants, and, in effect, traded as a single account. The advantage of these funds is that professionals make the trading decisions and your losses are limited to the amount you invest.

Professional management, however, does not guarantee success and is expensive. The typical commodity fund has steep sales fees plus annual management fees that can absorb anywhere from 10% to 20% of the fund's equity.

40

RISK

As shown in the first key, common stocks have on average proven to be excellent investments. With an average return of about 10%, common stocks have substantially outperformed corporate bonds and government securities. However, investors have to take into account the risks associated with these generous returns. In 1973–74, the Dow Jones Industrial Average dropped almost by half, from 1051.70 to 577.60. On October 19, 1987, the stock market collapsed, free-falling 508 points. This drop was 22.6%, even greater than the storied crash of October 29, 1929, when the DJIA lost 12.8% of its value. The stock market has never climbed upward in a smooth, predictable pattern. Periodically, there have been steep losses, jarring the confidence of nervous investors. As of 1994, there have been nine bear markets since 1945—defined as a drop of more than 20% in the Dow Jones Industrial Average. The last one occurred in 1990 with a drop of 21.2% in the 87-day period ending on October 11, 1990. Shareholders should not panic when these drops occur but look at them as potential opportunities.

Any investment always involves a tradeoff between risk and reward. The higher the reward an investor seeks, the greater the risks and uncertainties are likely to be. Stock pickers who beat the market in one period or another may have assumed great risk. Wise investors examine a strategy's level of risk in addition to its performance.

Although common stock has certainly proved to be rewarding for investors, there are risks and uncertainties, as discussed throughout this book. Your investment in common stock will fluctuate in price over a substantial range, especially if you hold it for several years. Don't expect to buy a stock at its low price for the year. Individual investors should be looking at a time horizon of three to five years. Ultimately, it will be the company's success in generating future earnings that will most influence the price of its stock. However, over any given period stock prices will fluctuate widely in response to company news, changes in industry conditions, the overall economic and political climate, unexpected events, and shifts in investor psychology.

Diversification. One proven method to reduce risk is for investors to diversify their holdings. This strategy doesn't mean that an investor must acquire 50 different stocks. Diversification depends not only on the number of stocks an investor owns but also on the types of stocks chosen. Investment risks are related to different economic variables such as consumer spending, business investment, and interest rates. If you have ten stocks, all in the utility industry, your portfolio is not diversified. These stocks will likely move together in response to changes in interest rates. Even a portfolio of stocks in the airline, auto, and steel industries achieves little in the way of diversification. All of these industries tend to be cyclical, so the stocks will be strongly influenced by changes in the business cycle. Investors should select stocks that don't follow the same pattern in response to changes in economic variables.

How many stocks comprise a relatively diversified portfolio? Martin Zweig in *Winning on Wall Street* says that investors with between $5000 and $20,000 should buy four or five stocks. A $50,000 portfolio should include eight or nine stocks. At $100,000, a dozen stocks is appropriate. Finally, at $250,000, he recommends a portfolio of roughly 20 stocks. Beyond that, for greater amounts of capital, he believes 33 stocks offer sufficient diversification.

41

DOLLAR COST AVERAGING

Peter Lynch, formerly portfolio manager of Fidelity Magellan, says that predicting the short-term direction of the market is futile. In his book *One Up on Wall Street,* he says that investors should concentrate on picking stocks and not attempt to predict the market as a whole. Over the long haul, it can be costly not to invest in stocks. The approximately 10% average yearly return since 1926 indicates how profitable stock investments are in the long run. Data for the Standard & Poor's 500-stock index since 1926 indicate that the odds of losing money in stocks over one year are around 30%. However, over ten years the risk of loss falls to just 4%.

Given the difficulty in predicting market turns, what strategy should an investor follow? One of the oldest and best of all formula plans is what is called dollar cost averaging, or the constant dollar plan. Dollar cost averaging requires that an investor commit a fixed amount of funds to stocks at specific time intervals—monthly, quarterly, or whatever period is most suitable to the investor's saving schedule. The technique is very mechanical at one level, requiring no forecast of the direction of the market. It is not a trading system but a long-term investment program.

Under this program the average cost of stocks in a portfolio should be less than the average market price of the stocks. This occurs because a constant amount of dollars purchases fewer shares at higher prices and more shares at lower prices. A simple example can illustrate this. Suppose you invest $500 every three months over the next year. Assume the price of your stock or mutual fund is $20 the first quarter, $10 the second, $20 the third, and $10 in the last quarter. The first quarter you acquire

25 shares at $20 each, for a total of $500. In the second quarter $500 buys you 50 shares. Then, at the end of the four quarters you will have acquired 150 shares with your $2000 investment, at an average cost of $13.33. However, during the year the average price of the stock was $15.

Although dollar cost averaging produces the best results with stocks that fluctuate substantially, the average investor should avoid stocks that are too volatile. The best policy is to buy high quality stocks that will continue to produce above average growth in revenue and earnings. Obviously, money cannot be made on a stock whose price moves continually downward.

The key to dollar cost averaging is that you have to have the patience to continue your contributions through good and bad market periods. To start with, you might invest $250 to $500 a month. The low cost of using mutual funds makes them good candidates for starting a program. Many of them feature automatic investment plans whereby an amount of money you specify is electronically transferred from your bank account and invested in a mutual fund on a regular basis.

42

401(K) RETIREMENT PLANS

Named after the section of the federal law, the 401(K) plan is an outstanding way to build a retirement nest egg. Most large companies sponsor 401(K) plans or similar tax-deferred plans, and many smaller companies have recently adopted them. The plan provides employees with an automatic way to save for retirement while reducing and deferring taxes. Everyone should take advantage of this benefit whenever it is available.

A 401(K) plan is a retirement plan that permits you to defer paying taxes on a part of your salary. This contribution is deducted from your salary and is not counted as part of your earnings when it comes time to determine your income tax. The maximum tax-free deduction is adjusted each year for inflation. In 1994, the maximum deduction was $9240. Taxpayers in the 28% bracket who made the maximum contribution of $9240 in 1994 will save $2587 in federal taxes.

What makes 401(K) plans even more enticing is that many companies match all or part of the employee contributions. They often, however, retain the option of claiming a portion of their matching contributions if the employee leaves the company within seven years.

As previously mentioned, the company chooses the investment options. The typical choices have included the employer's stock, a stock mutual fund, a fund combining stocks and bonds, and so-called guaranteed investment contracts (GICs), which are insurance contracts that pay a fixed rate of interest usually comparable to certificates of deposit.

However, we are moving from three or four options into an era where we will see eight or even twelve options as commonplace. New guidelines on 401(K) retirement plans, which took effect on January 1, 1994, call for a broad range of investment alternatives in various risk categories and continuing education for employees about how these investments work. Although the provisions are not mandatory, employers are generally observing them, largely because following the guidelines assures some legal protection against liability in case an investor loses money in a plan or makes poor choices.

Most people opt for the GIC option because they believe that these are the safest investments. That could be a big mistake. Locking in a guaranteed rate isn't worth giving up the potential price gains in common stock. Although GIC contracts now return about 7% annually, this return is considerably less than the 10% that stocks have historically returned.

Don't assume a 3% difference in return is insignificant. An investment of $10,000 with a return of 7% will grow to $54,270 when compounded over 25 years. In contrast, the same $10,000 when compounded at 10% over 25 years will grow to $108,350, about double the return at 7%.

Another mistake many employees make is to invest too much of their retirement plan money in their own company's stock. It is too risky to have your retirement nest egg too dependent upon a single stock.

Almost everyone agrees that investors who are saving for retirement should put some money in stocks. The question is how much? The mutual fund company T. Rowe Price recommends 80% for someone 25 years away from retirement. As you get older, you can gradually reduce the allocation. As retirement nears, you should shift some money out of the volatile stock category. For someone five years away from retirement, T. Rowe Price suggests a stock allocation of 40%.

If your plan has an international stock option, you should consider devoting 20% to 25% of your stock allocation to it. The markets outside the United States as a group have performed better than our market in 16 of the past 25 years through 1993. Many of these economies will continue to grow faster than our own economy. An exposure to international markets offers the likely possibility of increasing your return while reducing your risk.

You can begin making 401(K) withdrawals without penalty after age 59½ or when you retire or are permanently disabled. You must begin withdrawing your 401(K) money by age 70½. The money can be withdrawn in a lump sum, but many plans also provide for the purchase of an annuity or installment payments. In any case, the withdrawals are subject to regular income tax.

You can withdraw funds before age 59½ without penalty only if you are facing a financial hardship. To be eligible for early withdrawals, you may have to prove you have used up other financial resources before applying, and you can borrow only the amount you need. If you can't prove financial hardship, there is a 10% penalty for withdrawing funds before age 59½.

Many plans do permit borrowing. Loans can be made for any reason the employer allows, and are not recognized as withdrawals because the money is scheduled to be paid back. Before borrowing against the plan, however, ask what the interest rate on loans is and how long before you have to repay the loan. Remember, however, that dipping into 401(K) funds to pay short-term expenses can put your retirement nest egg at risk.

One of the most basic investment mistakes many employees make is not joining 401(K) plans. About one quarter of eligible employees are not participating. The younger employees are particularly apt to ignore these plans. They are making a serious error. The 401(K) plan is positively the best investment vehicle for an employee. You get automatic savings, your contribution and its earnings are tax deferred, and you get free money from your employer. A 401(K) plan will be the chief source of retirement income for many retirees in the future.

However small your contribution, everyone eligible should contribute to a 401(K) plan. Those employees who can afford to contribute the maximum should definitely do so. Take full advantage of this savings option before investing elsewhere.

43

INVESTMENT
CLUBS

One way for small investors to familiarize themselves with the stock market at little cost is to join an investment club. Investment clubs are groups of people—usually 10 to 20—who get together to learn investment principles, build an investment portfolio, and exchange information. Most of these groups join together once a month, deposit their monthly investment—typically $20 to $50—review studies of stocks presented by members, and select a stock in which to invest. The liquidating values of shares are computed regularly. One member is typically designated as an agent for the group. Any member who wants to withdraw from the club will receive the liquidating value of his/her shares.

Many of the clubs belong to the National Association of Investment Clubs (NAIC), a nonprofit organization whose annual dues are $35 per club plus $11 for each member of the club. For this price they provide a manual that gives complete instructions for organizing and operating an investment club and offers assistance in the evaluation of stocks. In addition, there is a monthly magazine, *Better Investing,* an excellent investment education publication.

The NAIC has three classes of membership: individual, investment club, and corporate. Currently, there are about 50,000 individual members, 226 corporate members, and 12,500 investment clubs with about 250,000 members. The average club is 8½ years old and has a portfolio worth about $100,000.

The NAIC lists four principles that provide a foundation for sound investing practice:

1. Invest a set sum once a month in common stocks, regardless of general market conditions. (This helps investors obtain lower average costs.)
2. Reinvest dividends and capital gains immediately. (Money grows faster if earnings are reinvested.)
3. Buy growth stocks—companies whose sales and earnings are increasing at an above average rate.
4. Invest in different fields. (Diversification helps spread both risk and opportunity.)

Information about the NAIC can be obtained from 711 West Thirteen Mile Road, Madison Heights, Michigan 48071, 810-583-6242.

American Association of Individual Investors. The American Association of Individual Investors (AAII) is an "independent, nonprofit corporation formed for the purpose of assisting individuals in becoming effective managers of their own assets through programs of education, information, and research." This estimable organization, composed of almost 200,000 members, is an invaluable source of information to all investors regardless of their expertise. The $49 annual membership fee includes a subscription to the monthly *AAII Journal* and the annual *The Individual Investor's Guide to No-Load Mutual Funds.*

The monthly magazine provides articles that are written by prominent practitioners and academicians in different areas and reflect the latest thinking in the field. The annual guide to no-load funds is a comprehensive, easy-to-read comparison of over 800 mutual funds. The data provided include a wide variety of risk and performance statistics of interest to investors.

In addition, the AAII has an investment home study program designed for those who want to enhance their understanding of investing. In ten lessons it explores the concepts, strategies, and analytical methods that are useful for successful investing and portfolio management. The program costs $55 for members, and updates and revisions are sent free to members. Information about the AAII can be obtained from 625 North Michigan Avenue, Suite 1900, Chicago, Illinois 60611, 312-280-0170.

44

INVESTMENT SCAMS

Every year the financial media reports on some investment scam that has duped unwary investors. Investors continually put their money in scams that clearly ought to arouse suspicion. In 1994, thousands of investors lost millions of dollars while buying investments in second mortgages, stamps, coins, and wireless cable. How did they get bilked? They listened to so-called free advice offered by investment-talk radio shows pitching dubious products instead of offering objective advice. The free advice cost many people their life savings, according to federal prosecutors.

Ponzi schemes. A 30-year-old immigrant, Charles Ponzi, etched his name in the annals of history in 1920 when he made an offer thousands of investors could not refuse—a 50% return in just six weeks. By the time the scheme began to unravel six months later, Ponzi had pocketed $10 million. His name has become synonymous with confidence games in which some early investors earn excellent returns, paid off with funds obtained from later participants in a scheme, who lose everything. Variations on the Ponzi scheme have duped investors over and over again. When the demand for new participants exhausts the supply, the Ponzi pyramid collapses, crushing the hopes of its "investors." These schemes are illegal in most states.

Stock scams. Any investment that guarantees an unusually high rate of return should be regarded with extreme caution. The penny stock market has been a continuing source of headaches to state securities regulators. Investors are continually bilked by swindlers who prey on those who substitute greed for sound judgment.

The emergence of computerized dialing and cheap long-distance phone rates has allowed smooth-talking brokers working out of "boiler rooms" to contact millions of people. They offer stock in small companies for a few cents per share, promising nuge profits in a short time. Investors should be wary of the penny stock market.

Of course, there are legitimate penny stock offerings, but these are only for speculators who are able to absorb the inevitable losses in the hope of finding a big winner. Penny stock quotes will not be found in newspapers but are published in "pink sheets," which are available at brokerage firms.

Phony financial planners. A growing number of crooks are exploiting individuals concerned about their financial well-being by selling them bogus investments and worthless counseling. Most of this fraud is perpetrated not by financial planners, but by frauds posing as financial planners. Investors can reduce their chances of falling prey to a charlatan by checking the backgrounds of financial planners and other investment professionals with the securities office of their state. For information on whom to call, phone the North American Securities Association in Washington, D.C. (202-737-0900). For information about past disciplinary actions against brokers or their firms, investors can call (800-289-9999).

45

INVESTMENT STRATEGIES

Are there certain stratagems investors can follow to generate stock market gains? Yes, there are. However, investors should remember not to follow any strategy blindly. Ultimately, the important point is the factors that drive these strategies. Investors should understand the nature of the stocks they own and the specific reasons for holding the stocks.

Low P/E ratios. Academic research has found that low P/E stocks consistently produce larger long-term returns than high P/E stocks. David Dreman, in his book *The Contrarian Investment Strategy,* states that, in the aggregate, companies for which the strongest growth is projected don't meet market expectations of earnings growth, and the companies with supposedly the worst prospects often don't do as poorly as investors anticipate. Investors who follow this strategy need to observe the following guidelines:

1. Determine that the company's financial condition is strong. A low P/E might be justified by the market's concern about the risk associated with a company's large debt position.
2. Look for solid earnings growth (at least 15% per year over the last five years).
3. Be cautious about cyclical companies. A low P/E may reflect the fact that earnings are at a cyclical peak.

Look for small companies. Stocks with market capitalizations (price times number of shares outstanding) between $20 million and $100 million tend to outperform larger stocks after adjusting for risk. The earnings of smaller companies can grow faster than those of larger companies, because they are starting from a far smaller base. A more aggressive investor might want to include a few emerging growth companies in his/her portfolio. Some guidelines to follow:

1. Look for earnings growth of 20% to 25% over the last five years.
2. Determine if the company can maintain or increase this growth rate.
3. Make certain that its debt load is reasonable. Small companies with large debt can get into serious financial difficulties if an economic downturn occurs.

Low institutional ownership. Common stocks that are widely held by institutions tend to not do as well as stocks with little or no institutional ownership. The best time to buy a stock is before the institutions become attracted to it and run up the price.

Insider buying. Companies that report a high level of insiders' (defined as officers, directors, or a stockholder who owns more than 10% of the stock) purchases perform better than firms reporting heavy sales by insiders. The SEC requires the disclosure of this information which is carried in *Barron's, The Wall Street Journal, and Investor's Business Daily.*

Avoid penny stocks. This market is fraught with stock manipulation and fraud. Buying these stocks is more akin to gambling than investing.

QUESTIONS AND ANSWERS

What is the difference between a primary market for common stock and a secondary market?

The sale of new securities to raise funds is a primary market transaction. The proceeds of the sale of these securities represent new capital for the firm. New issues are typically underwritten by investment bankers who acquire the total issue from the company. They then resell these securities in smaller units to individual and institutional investors.

After a new issue of securities is sold in the primary market, subsequent trades of the security take place in the secondary market. The secondary market is vital because it provides liquidity to investors who acquire securities in the primary market.

What is the major reason for the existence of regional stock exchanges? How do they differ from national stock exchanges?

Regional stock exchanges trade the securities of local companies that are not large enough to qualify for listing on one of the national exchanges. As a result, the listing requirements are not as stringent as those of the New York Stock Exchange or the American Stock Exchange. In addition, regional exchanges list firms that are listed on one of the national exchanges for brokers who are not members of a national exchange. This dual listing permits local brokerage firms that are not members of the New York Stock Exchange to trade shares of dual-listed stock using their membership on a regional exchange. Membership on a regional exchange is typically much less expensive than on the national exchanges.

What is the relationship between NASDAQ and the over-the-counter (OTC) market?

The OTC market is the largest segment of the secondary market in terms of the number of securities (nearly 20,000). Although OTC stocks represent many small and unseasoned companies, the range of securities traded is very wide. This market is a negotiated market where investors directly negotiate purchases and sales through dealers.

The NASDAQ system is a computerized system providing current bid and asked prices on over 5000 of the most widely traded OTC securities. Through a dealer, a broker can instantly discover the bid and asked quotations offered by all dealers making a market in a stock. The broker can then contact the dealer offering the best price and negotiate a trade directly.

Are there any drawbacks to following the Dow Jones Industrial Average (DJIA) as a measure of market performance? Are there other stock market indicators?

The DJIA is the most widely followed barometer of stock price movements. However, the index is made up of only 30 large "blue-chip" companies. In addition, the DJIA is price weighted, meaning that the component stock prices are added together and the result is divided by another figure, the divisor. As a result, a high-priced stock has a greater effect on the index than a low-priced stock. A significant fluctuation in the price of one or several of the stocks in the index can distort the average.

After the DJIA, Standard & Poor's (S&P) 500 Stock Index is the most widely followed stock index. On a daily basis, its movement is more representative of the movement of the stock market as a whole than the DJIA because of its larger sample size and the fact that the index is market weighted. In a market-weighted average, both the price and number of shares outstanding enter into the computation.

Why should an investor hold a diversified portfolio? What is the simplest way to diversify?

Diversification can substantially reduce the risk associated with investments. Diversification can be stated simply as not putting all your eggs in one basket. An effectively diversified portfolio reduces risk without cutting long-run average return. In selecting stocks, then, investors should be careful to choose stocks whose risks are related to different economic, political, and social factors.

A diversified portfolio is very difficult to achieve when funds are limited. For those investors with limited funds, a mutual fund offers the opportunity to participate in an investment pool that can contain hundreds of different securities.

What is a growth stock?

A growth stock is defined as a company whose earnings have significantly outstripped the earnings of other companies in the past and are expected to do so in the future. These companies tend to reinvest a large part of their earnings and thus pay a relatively low (or no) dividend to shareholders. Investors who purchase these shares are more concerned with the appreciation in the market price of the stock than they are with the receipt of cash dividends.

Since these stocks provide little income, they are dependent upon high growth rates to sustain a high stock price. If these growth rates do not materialize, the stock can fall dramatically. As a consequence, investors in growth stocks should be aware of the greater risks associated with the possibility of earning the superior returns.

What is the difference between a bull market and a bear market? What are the implications of each to the investor?

A bull market is a prolonged rise in the price of stocks; a bear market is a prolonged decline in the price of stocks. Stock market movements are extremely important to investors. Historical studies indicate that 60% of stock price movements are directly related to movements in the overall market; 30% to 35% are related to sector or group movements and only 5% are related to individual stock movements.

Because stock prices have generally risen over time, bull markets predominate over bear markets. In fact, the market typically rises two out of every three years. Although bear markets tend to be of substantially shorter duration than bull markets, the decline can be steep. Even excluding the crash of 1929–32, when stock prices plunged 89%, the average bear market loss is about 30% from peak to trough.

How does a warrant differ from a call option? Which is riskier?

Warrants are options to acquire a fixed number of common shares at a predetermined price during a specified time period. The definition is similar to that of a call option with some key differences. First, warrants are issued by the company that issued the stock rather than by an independent option writer. Second, the life of a warrant is usually much longer than the life of a call option; the typical term of warrants may vary from two years to perpetuity.

For investors, warrants are pure speculations. Leverage works both ways. Warrant prices go up or down faster than the underlying stock. In this sense they are similar to options. Their advantage over options is that the longer period to expiration gives the investor the opportunity to speculate on a company over a longer term.

What is the difference between an open-end and closed-end investment company?

Two basic types of funds exist: closed-end mutual funds and open-end mutual funds. A closed-end mutual fund is an investment company with a fixed number of shares that trades on an exchange or over-the-counter. Similarly to common stock, the price of these funds changes as demand for the shares changes. Many of these stock funds trade at a discount from their net asset value.

Open-end mutual funds, by far the most popular type of fund, issue or redeem shares at the net asset value of the portfolio. Unlike closed-end funds, the number of shares is not fixed but increases as investors purchase more shares. These shares are not traded on any market and are always worth total assets minus total liabilities, divided by the number of shares.

What are redemption fees and 12b-1 plans?

Until recently, mutual funds were either load or no-load. But today, fee structures are made more complex and often are not made clear to investors. Among these fees are redemption fees, also called contingent deferred sales charges or back-end loads. This fee is charged if an investor sells his/her shares, usually within a fixed period. It may be a flat percentage of the sales price or may be based on a sliding scale, say 5% the first year, declining in steps to 0% in year 5.

Under the controversial 12b-1 plans, the fund can charge a fee to pay for its marketing and promotion costs. A 12b-1 fee can be levied on the full value of the investment each year or on the original value of the investment.

All funds also charge a management fee in order to compensate the asset managers for their services. These fees range from around 0.5% of the funds assets to 2% or even more.

Information on fees and other expense data is available on page 2 of every mutual fund prospectus. Investors should always read this page before purchasing a mutual fund.

Investors do not always get what they pay for. Thus, the funds that charge the highest fees do not necessarily increase in value faster than the "cheaper" funds.

How does the Securities and Exchange Commission (SEC) serve the investor?

The SEC was established by Congress to administer federal laws that seek to provide protection for investors. The overriding purpose of these laws is to ensure the integrity of the securities markets by requiring full disclosure of material facts related to securities offered to the public for sale.

The SEC does not insure investors. Nor does it prevent the sale of securities in risky, poorly managed, or unprofitable companies. Rather, registration with the SEC is designed to provide adequate and accurate disclosure of required material facts about the company and securities it proposes to sell. A portion of the information included in the registration statement is included in a prospectus that is prepared for public distribution.

The SEC requires the continual disclosure of company activities through annual, quarterly, and special reports. Form 10-K is the annual report, which contains a myriad of financial data in addition to nonfinancial information such as the names of corporate officers and directors and the extent of their ownership. Form 10-Q is the quarterly report, which contains abbreviated financial and nonfinancial information. Form 8-K is a report of material events or corporate changes deemed of importance to the shareholders or to the SEC. All of these can be obtained from the company or the SEC.

Does a balance sheet disclose the current market value of assets?

Generally, the answer is no. Items reflected under property, plant, and equipment are shown at their original cost less the total depreciation recognized on the asset (called accumulated depreciation). The current market value of these assets is not reflected in the financial statements. For many corporations, the amount shown for property, plant, and equipment in the balance sheet is but a small percentage of the current market value of these assets.

The balance sheet also fails to disclose certain assets of vital importance to the corporation. For example, the value of a corporation's human resources is not reflected in the balance sheet. Additionally, the value of brand names is often not disclosed, or if disclosed, is shown at unamortized cost, which has no relationship to current market value. In recent years, the purpose of many takeovers has been to acquire valuable brand names.

GLOSSARY

Arbitrage profiting from differences in price when the same security is traded on two or more markets.

Balance sheet financial statement showing a firm's assets, liabilities, and owners' equity as of a particular date.

Bear person who believes that stock prices will drop.

Bear market prolonged period of declining prices. These periods usually last at least several months, and sometimes a year or more.

Big Board traders' term for the New York Stock Exchange.

Bull person who believes that stock prices will rise.

Bull market prolonged increase in the prices of securities. These markets usually last at least several months, sometimes several years.

Callable the option of a company to call in a security and redeem it for cash.

Call option right of a buyer to purchase a specified quantity of a security interest at a fixed price at any time during the life of the option.

Common stock fractional shares of ownership in a firm.

Convertible security bond or share of preferred stock that can be exchanged into a specified amount of common stock at a specified price.

Discount rate rate of interest charged by the Federal Reserve to member banks.

Diversification an attempt to reduce the overall risk of a portfolio by owning different securities rather than concentrating all one's money in one or two investments.

Dividend reimbursement plan automatic reinvestment of shareholder dividends in more shares of the company's stock.

Dividends payments made by a corporation to its stockholders.

Earnings per share amount of net income attributable to each share of common stock.

Federal Reserve Board consists of seven members who oversee the formulation of monetary policy and control of the money supply.

Financial leverage accelerative effect of debt on financial returns.

Financial ratios indicators of a company's financial performance and position.

401(K) plan investment that allows an employee to contribute pretax dollars up to a stated limit to a company pool, which is invested with the capital and earnings compounding on a tax-deferred basis until the employee retires or leaves the company.

Fundamental analysis process of estimating a security's value by analyzing the basic financial and economic facts about the company that issues the security.

Golden parachute lucrative compensation guaranteed top executives in the event of a takeover.

Greenmail purchase by a corporation of its own stock from a potential acquirer at a price substantially greater than the market price. In exchange, the acquirer agrees to drop the takeover bid.

Hedging actions taken by investors to reduce a possible loss.

Income statement financial statement showing a firm's revenues and expenses over a period of time.

Initial Public Offering corporation's first offering of its own stock to the public.

Investment banking industry that specializes in assisting business firms and governments in marketing new securities.

Junk bond a high-risk, high-yield bond (less than BBB rating), generally issued either by a new company or to fund a corporate takeover.

Leveraged buyout process of buying a corporation's stock with borrowed money, then repaying at least part of the debt from the corporation's assets.

Liquidity the ease with which an asset can be converted into cash, reflecting a firm's ability to meet its short-term obligations.

Load fund type of mutual fund where the buyer must pay a sales fee, or commission, on top of the price.

Margin trading using borrowed funds for trading; trading on credit, as governed by Federal Reserve and stock exchange regulations.

Market efficiency description of how prices in competitive markets react to new information.

Merger combination of two or more firms into one.

Monetary policy actions by the Federal Reserve to control the money supply, bank lending, and interest rates.

NASDAQ National Association of Securities Dealers Automated Quotations; a computerized communications network that provides quotations (bid and asked prices) on stock.

No-load fund type of mutual fund for which no commission is charged to make a purchase.

OTC market Over-the-counter market; trades securities through a centralized computer telephone network that links dealers across the U.S.

Poison pill tactic used by corporations to defend against unfriendly takeovers, generally by making a takeover more expensive.

Portfolio an investor's collection of securities.

Price/earnings (P/E) ratio ratio of a share's market price to a company's earnings per share.

Prospectus formal written offer to sell securities; includes audited financial statements and other information about the company.

Put option right of a buyer to sell a specified quantity of a security interest at a fixed price at any time during the life of the option.

Registration statement contains a firm's financial statements and other information that is filed with the Securities and Exchange Commission each time a new security is offered to the public.

Secondary offering public sale of previously issued securities owned by large investors.

Short sale sale of a borrowed security with the intention of purchasing it later at a lower price.

Statement of cash flows financial statement showing a firm's cash receipts and cash payments over a period of time.

Stock dividend pro rata distribution of additional shares of stock to stockholders.

Stock market averages average of the market prices of a specified number of stocks.

Stock split issuance of new shares of stock to stockholders in proportion to the shares they already own.

Stock table summary of the trading activity of individual securities.

Technical analysis process of predicting future stock price movements by analyzing the historical movement of stock prices and supply and demand forces that affect those prices.

Tender offer offer by one firm to the stockholders of another firm to purchase a specified number of shares at a specified price within a specified time period.

Underwriter investment banker who, alone or as a member of an underwriting group or syndicate, agrees to purchase a new issue of securities from an issuer and distribute it to investors.

Uptick trade transactions executed at a price higher than the previous trade.

Warrant option to buy a specified number of common shares at a predetermined price within a fixed time period.

White knight person or corporation who saves a corporation from a hostile takeover by taking it over on more favorable terms.

INDEX